Making Good Return

Making Good Return

Biblical Wisdom on Honoring Aging Parents

Kathleen B. Nielson

P.O. BOX 817 • PHILLIPSBURG • NEW JERSEY 08865-0817

A Scripture quotation from the New Testament uses the ESV's alternate, footnoted translation of *adelphoi* ("brothers and sisters").

Italics within Scripture quotations indicate emphasis added.

Cover design by Jelena Mirkovic

Printed in the United States of America

Library of Congress Cataloging-in-Publication Data

Names: Nielson, Kathleen Buswell, author.
Title: Making good return : biblical wisdom on honoring aging parents / Kathleen B. Nielson.
Description: Phillipsburg, New Jersey : P&R Publishing, [2024] | Summary: "Addressing spiritual realities and practical difficulties, Nielson delves into five rich scriptural truths about aging and the aged to shape our mindset and approach as we care for elderly parents"-- Provided by publisher.
Identifiers: LCCN 2024004109 | ISBN 9798887790282 (paperback) | ISBN 9798887790299 (epub)
Subjects: LCSH: Aging parents--Care--Religious aspects--Christianity. | Adult children of aging parents--Religious life. | Aging--Religious aspects--Christianity. | Caring--Religious aspects--Christianity.
Classification: LCC BV4910.9 .N54 2024 | DDC 248.8/5--dc23/eng/20240222
LC record available at https://lccn.loc.gov/2024004109

With thanksgiving for my parents,
John and LaVon Buswell

Contents

Introduction

It is dangerous to write a book about something you're still in the middle of. For several years after conceiving the idea of this book, I kept putting off the writing. When my dear mother had gone to heaven and my care for my parents was complete, I thought, then would be the perfect time to write—when I had learned all the lessons I could learn. We see better in hindsight. When my mother turned ninety-six, however, I suddenly realized that I was fast getting older as well . . . and the writing began.

In the process, I've confronted the magnitude of the subject and concluded it was good to go ahead and write, for there is no end to the lessons we caregivers can learn; in any case, one book can cover only a bit. It was good to begin writing also because, as I'm still taking care of Mom, I have live empathy for those who, like me, are in the process of being schooled by God in the art of caring for aging loved ones.

I have not counted the number of people who have commented to me on the need to address this topic, but it's been overwhelming —and the comments have come with a definite urgency. Many adult children like me (averaging fifty- or sixty-something years old) are being called up to parent-care duty and feel the need for advice and help, especially as a similar call from children and grandchildren often pulls from the other side.

This situation will only intensify in coming years, as we baby boomers begin to crowd the ranks of the elderly. The need to help and encourage caregivers is urgent indeed, not only in the general public but specifically in the church, for the Bible speaks strongly to the subject of God's care and our care for the elderly ones in our midst.

This is a book written from a Christian perspective, acknowledging the God-breathed truths of the Old and New Testaments concerning human beings created by God in the beginning and headed to meet God face-to-face in the end. At the center of these biblical truths is the Lord Jesus Christ, the Son of God who came to earth to save us through his death on the cross, bearing our sins, and his resurrection from the dead.

The redemptive story of God's calling out a people for himself through Jesus Christ is not just the context of a Christian's thinking about care for the aging; it is at the very heart of the matter—as is the case with all parts of life. As I have written I have been continually aware of the many people, including many friends, whose aging loved ones are not believers in the Lord Jesus; I have aimed to write with acknowledgment of our many different contexts and situations, as well as with wisdom concerning care for the elderly that takes eternity into account.

This is not a "how-to" book that covers topics like writing wills and choosing long-term care facilities. Many practical details are indeed addressed, but those details come mainly in the process of exploring biblical principles and their real-life implications. In considering how to put this book together, I searched the Bible with an eye to this theme of caring for aging parents and the elderly among us—and I was amazed by the volume and the richness of what I found.

The book's structure, then, grew from what the Scriptures have to say regarding this topic, and it is organized into what I've called five "big biblical truths" about the process of aging and elder care. Each of the five truths comes with a related response. The chapters are ordered in pairs, with the first of the pair presenting the biblical truth and the second fleshing out the related response to that truth.

Many people helped me write this book. In the early stages, I requested thoughts and stories from a group of friends who have firsthand experience in caring for aging parents. They responded with a host of wise, thoughtful suggestions and ideas—and moving accounts of their own experiences, many of which are very different from mine. These friends are not named as their contributions are folded into the chapters, but I thank each of them for making the book much more rich and true than it would have been without their help. I thank my family for living out the realities of this book as we have together watched over aging parents and grandparents. This book's topic involves not just individuals but also families. As always, my husband, Niel, is my most loved and true critic, in the best sense of the word.

The book's title comes from Paul's first epistle to Timothy, a letter in which the older apostle is guiding his younger coworker in wise and godly church leadership. In his instructions regarding various segments of the congregation, Paul writes that widows are to be honored and cared for not first by the church but by their own children and grandchildren, who are "to show godliness to their own household and to make some return to their parents, for this is pleasing in the sight of God" (1 Tim. 5:4). This book asks how we grown children can "make return" to our aging parents in a way that is pleasing in God's sight.

It's an urgent question. I'm certainly not finished learning how to answer it. Even in the middle of trying to figure it out, though, we can pause, look up, look into the Bible, and better understand how to please God as we care for our aging loved ones. By God's grace, we can make progress in making good return to our parents. That is what this book aims to help us do.

1

God Sovereignly Ordains Our Aging

As the sun sets, I pull up to the front of the retirement community in which my mother has lived for several years now. It has been a full day, the contours of which I know well, as I make the monthly trip to visit Mom: catch the early flight from Chicago, rejoice when the rental car is waiting for me in Harrisburg, Pennsylvania, then navigate the highway and finally the winding roads through rich farmland and Amish homesteads with black and white clothes hanging out on the line no matter the season. I know and like knowing how the Lancaster County farms and fields look in the different seasons, from dead-looking brown stubby stretches and huddled, muddy cattle to swaying, tall green corn and cows with calves scattered on gentle hills.

Before I go in (where I will be confronted immediately with at least a dozen urgent needs that Mom has been waiting for me to help with), I stop, take a breath, gather my thoughts, and say a prayer.

This book is an extension of that moment of preparation. Before we walk in to the dwelling places of the elderly, before we make aged parents the objects of our care and the subjects of our conversation, let's stop, consider, and above all look up to the eternal Lord God, who oversees us human creatures from the beginning to the end of our days on this earth. Let's try to see what he sees. And then let's go in.

The Foundation of God's Word

But how can we survey the landscape of a human life the way God does? In this book, we will peer into a certain part of this landscape—the part farthest away, where clear lines gradually blur into the distance ahead. To those of us who are not yet there, it's the part where the figures and the action seem to get smaller. If we're going to care for the ones who inhabit that portion of the landscape, we need to understand what life there is like. The ones who are there don't always have words to explain it to us, and we do not always have ears to hear. How shall we gain a true perspective on the experience of aging and on the best ways of reaching out to those who are walking on ahead through the territory of old age?

The Bible gives us words we can trust—God's inspired words of truth concerning the human beings he created. There is no other place to start than the foundation of God's Word. What do the Scriptures reveal concerning those later years of life, when a person has lived "seventy, or even by reason of strength eighty" years (Ps. 90:10)—or, in the case of a growing number today, ninety years?

Only the eternal Lord God who created the universe (and each of us) truly sees the whole span of a human life. In one sense, he is so big and powerful that we humans are like grasshoppers, says the prophet Isaiah, to the one "who sits above the circle of the earth" (Isa. 40:22). Isaiah uses vivid pictures—we are not just grasshoppers but *grass*: "All flesh is grass, and all its beauty is like the flower of the field" (40:6). We are so small and so quickly here and gone.

Part of Isaiah's point, however, is that the Creator God does see us little fleeting creatures. Only the greatest can see the smallest. We must not think that God does not see us, from birth to death and down to every particle of our skin and bones and blood and organs—and soul. Isaiah asks why God's people say that their way is hidden from the Lord:

> Have you not known? Have you not heard?
> The LORD is the everlasting God,
>   the Creator of the ends of the earth.
> He does not faint or grow weary;
>   his understanding is unsearchable. (40:28)

This is where we must start, in order to get God's view: with *him*, in all his unsearchable understanding. He sees and sovereignly rules over the ends of the earth he made.

It is humbling and comforting to find that this great Lord God pays a good deal of attention, in his written revelation, to old age; he speaks clearly into this part of our human experience. God's Word on aging shows us a tender and merciful aspect of his heart for the human creatures he made. As we listen, we are blessed and instructed—not only in learning to care well for aging loved ones but also in preparing ourselves, by God's grace, to live as godly residents in the territory of the elderly. Most of us will move in there, far away as it seems while we inhabit the earlier stages of life. It will be best to have staked out the territory.

Aging Occurs under God's Sovereign Rule

Of our five big biblical truths about old age, first and foremost we must consider this one: *aging occurs under God's sovereign rule*. Of course it does, a Christian might say: the Scriptures reveal a sovereign Lord God who created us and who eternally rules over all his creation. The Bible encourages us to consider God's sovereignty in all things—in nature, for example, as he orders the seasons, the planets, the rain; in the rise and fall of kings and nations; and in the measure of a human life from beginning to end.

We know that the Lord orders our beginnings, from Adam and Eve through every one of their descendants, each of whom he knits together in their mother's womb (see Ps. 139:13). We also know the Lord orders the end of our days in these present mortal bodies; each day of our lives has already been written in God's book (see Ps. 139:16). The spans of our little lives are part of God's big story. It follows that, in order to grasp the significance of our own beginnings and endings, we must pay attention to the beginning and ending of the big story of the Bible. Our stories have full meaning only when understood in light of God's story.

We cannot imagine how the days in the garden of Eden might have unfolded had Adam and Eve not sinned and brought God's declared punishment of death on themselves and consequently on the entire human race (see Gen. 2:17; Rom. 5:12). What would "aging" have meant without sin and all its consequences? What would have been the experience through time of God's people living perfectly under God's rule?

But that's not how God's story goes. The first book of the Bible quickly tells us how sin broke into God's perfect creation, bringing with it death, both physical and spiritual—alienation on every level from our holy Creator. It tells us more, however. As early as Genesis 3:15, God makes a promise that points to the defeat of sin and death: the evil Serpent will be crushed by the offspring of the woman. God's sovereign plan for his people to live under his rule would not be thwarted but would come about through a Redeemer who would conquer death. From the foundation of the world, God willed to create a people who would live with him forever through the work of Jesus Christ his Son, who became flesh and died, bearing the full punishment of sin in the place of sinners (see Eph. 1:3–10).

The big story of the Bible unfolds according to God's promises. The plan of salvation was accomplished victoriously; in Christ, death was defeated at the cross and the empty tomb. But the story is not over. We human beings remain in this fallen world, in these dying bodies, awaiting the completion of redemptive history when Jesus Christ comes again to claim his people, from Adam and Eve down through the last believer to be born. In that great day of resurrection, all dead bodies will rise from the grave, "some to everlasting life, and some to shame and everlasting contempt" (Dan. 12:2; see also John 5:28–29). At the final judgment, death itself will be thrown into the lake of fire (see Rev. 20:14). The prophet Isaiah tells us that the Lord "will swallow up death forever" (25:8). There will be a new heaven and a new earth, and new resurrected bodies for the people of God who live there with him: God's plan will not be thwarted. The very end of the story is good, and it reaches out into eternity.

We embodied human beings are taking part in a huge story of redemption, a story sovereignly decreed by the Lord God for his glory alone. The Bible reveals this sovereign God to be just and merciful, ordering the span of each life and all lives as part of his great redemptive plan, with Jesus Christ at its center. The bodily beginning—and end—of each human life is necessarily linked to God's larger story, which is moving inexorably toward the glorious conclusion he has sovereignly set in place.

Focusing In: Aging and Death within the Story

The point here is to ask how we view the earthly endings of our little stories in light of the big story. By "endings" I mean to include not just death but also the aging process that leads to death. Perhaps that is the first admission we need to make about aging as we know it: it is the precursor of death. It is linked to death. Recently, I heard a woman claim that aging is a good thing, a beautiful thing, part of the "flow of nature." Now, we will talk about how the Lord means to make the aging process beautiful—and he does. He redeems everything. But in itself the aging process is essentially the decay of the body that leads to death.

My husband and I are together enjoying the white hairs of old age. My mother has the most beautiful head of pure white hair; she dyed her hair for years, but now she takes a certain pleasure in the whiteness of her fluffy bob. As Proverbs says, "Gray hair is a crown of glory; it is gained in a righteous life" (16:31). But we should be careful to distinguish between the whiteness that symbolically points to the dignity and value of a wise older person, on the one hand, and the whiteness that literally indicates a decline in the pigment of our hair follicles, on the other. Our pigment cells die, so that as we get older we have less and less of the living stuff that gave our hair its color. The autumn leaves that turn brilliant shades and fall to the ground have dried up and died.

Aging leads to death, and death is a result of the fall. Aging, then, is not good in itself; rather, it is a consequence of sin in this fallen world. It is given to us by a sovereign God who kept his word to Adam: death would result from disobedience. We must understand the process of aging as part of the Bible's big story—a story directed not by a beneficent, neutral, or even random natural force, but by the Lord God. It is a story that comes not in a steady unending flow or in happy cycles but in the archetypal shape that shows itself in stories of all places and times: a distinct beginning (creation), a clear crisis (the fall), a shining climax (the cross and the resurrection), and a perfectly resolved denouement (the return of Christ).

As we believers live in our part of the story, looking ahead to the resolution of our Savior's return, God's Word enables us to hold the whole biblical framework in our minds. We can move with hope toward the very end because of the victory over sin and death accomplished by Jesus our Redeemer. The promise of the big story's end is magnificent because he will make new all the wonders of creation we glimpse in the story's beginning.

But waiting for that end is difficult because of the effects of the fall. To grapple with the reality of aging is to acknowledge that part of the story. This acknowledgment is a crucial starting point as we approach the subject of aging. We will hear voices around us assuming many unbiblical starting points—one of them being that aging and death are natural and good. Another is the assumption that we human beings are in control of the aging process.

Usurping God's Sovereignty

We human beings desperately want to write our own stories, including the later chapters. We desire sovereignty over the endings of our lives in these mortal bodies. God has put in us a strong instinct to live; we most often try to avoid death at all costs because we fear death as the enemy it is, a fierce foe that would take away everything we have. Much of the advertising that bombards us today plays to these desires and fears: if we can just protect ourselves with the best available exercise routines, safety measures, medical care, beauty products, and retirement plans, we can almost expect never to face the horror of death.

Almost. These protections can (sometimes) dramatically extend our days, but they do not ultimately succeed. The most obtrusive and unavoidable giveaway to this truth is the process of aging. No beauty cream can erase all the wrinkles. No amount of exercise or surgery can keep a ninety-something-year-old body as strong as it was in the prime of life (whatever that is). We age. Everyone knows it. And we age under the sovereign hand of a God who has judged this sinful world with the punishment of death. Aging is one sign of the futility and corruption to which the whole creation was subjected by God (see Rom. 8:20–21). The denial of these biblical truths most often involves denying sin, and it ultimately involves denying God.

The attempt to establish our own sovereignty over death takes many forms: we can call it our enemy and try to defeat it, but we can also call it our friend and invite it in. To treat aging and death as "natural" is perhaps a first step in the latter direction. But such steps lead us to call evil good in all kinds of ways. To understand the extreme danger inherent in this view, all we have to do is listen to the way practices like abortion and euthanasia are lauded in the public sphere as good ways to increase human self-determination and happiness. We fool ourselves in the most deadly way when we dress up death as our ally, our comforter, our friend—rather than acknowledging death as God's punishment for our sin.

I sat with friends in Switzerland not long ago as they discussed the increasingly common practice of "exiting," that is, choosing (legally) to end one's life. All one needs is a letter from a medical professional, and those letters are easy to obtain. Those who exit are seeking peace as they embrace death. In refusing to accept God's sovereign gift of life, however, they are rejecting the sovereign God himself, who made a way for us to know peace with him forever, through his Son.

Until the Lord comes, we will all experience the moment of death, when our physical eyes close and our spiritual eyes are opened to the realities of the spiritual world. On this side of the great divide, the quiet of a dead body doesn't tell the story; we cannot see and know what that person sees and knows. God has revealed the story in the Scriptures and ultimately in his Son, who took on a body to die and save us from death. We cannot see him yet, either, in his glorious resurrected body, but we can believe the Bible and the true story of human history it tells. In that story, death is a grievous and ugly enemy that has been defeated by our beautiful Savior and eternal Friend. In the end, every eye will see the Lord Jesus (see Rev. 1:7).

Responding Humbly to a Sovereign God

These truths are both somber and glorious—and they are good. We are not writing our own little stories, including the final chapters, thank God. According to Scripture, a good and merciful God numbers our days as he directs human history for his redemptive purposes.

We know that human beings once lived much longer than we do today: Adam lived 930 years—and Methuselah a record 969 (see Gen. 5:5, 27). As evil multiplied on the earth, God limited the human life span, declaring, "My Spirit shall not abide in man forever, for he is flesh: his days shall be 120 years" (Gen. 6:3). After that declaration, some people still lived long lives: Noah was 600 at the time of the flood and lived 350 years afterward (see Gen. 7:6; 9:28). But the numbers gradually decreased: Abraham lived 175 years, Moses 120 years, David 70 years (see Gen. 25:7; Deut. 34:7; 2 Sam. 5:4; 1 Kings 2:10–11). The almighty Lord has numbered our days in this sinful world; that limitation is surely meant to turn us to him in humility as we sense the brevity of our lives under the hand of a sovereign and eternal Maker and Judge.

I was reminded of an episode in the life of King David as I read through a lovely, wise book by Derek Prime.[1] In Prime's alphabet of wisdom on aging, *A* is for *acceptance*, as illustrated by the story of Barzillai the Gileadite, a wealthy friend of David's who brings David and his men shelter and provision in the wilderness during Absalom's rebellion. When peace is restored, David invites the elderly Barzillai to return to Jerusalem with him and enjoy his kingly provision. We can learn much from Barzillai's response:

> How many years have I still to live, that I should go up with the king to Jerusalem? I am this day eighty years old. Can I discern what is pleasant and what is not? Can your servant taste what he eats or what he drinks? Can I still listen to the voice of singing men and singing women? Why then should your servant be an added burden to my lord the king? Your servant will go a little way over the Jordan with the king. Why should the king

1. Derek Prime, *A Good Old Age: An A to Z of Loving and Following the Lord Jesus in Later Years* (2017; repr., Leyland, UK: 10Publishing, 2021). See pages 15–21 for Prime's discussion of the story of David and Barzillai.

> repay me with such a reward? Please let your servant return, that I may die in my own city near the grave of my father and my mother. (2 Sam. 19:34–37)

Barzillai then offers for one of his men to go with David in his place, and David accepts, kisses and blesses his friend, and leaves him. It's all told matter-of-factly. Barzillai (and David, apparently) accepted his lot—not with bitterness but with a realism that acknowledged the truth of his condition: he was eighty, and his taste and vision and hearing were failing. He was still actively helping others, but he understood that he would die relatively soon. And he knew that his own home would be the best place for him. We have to admire his humble, honest acceptance of his condition.

Then there is King Hezekiah, who wasn't so accepting. At one point in his reign as king of Judah, he became sick and "was at the point of death"; the prophet Isaiah even came and told him to set his house in order, for he was to die (Isa. 38:1). But Hezekiah wept and pleaded with the Lord, and God sent an answer, again through Isaiah: God said he would heal Hezekiah and add fifteen years to his life—and also deliver him and the city of Jerusalem from the attacking Assyrian army (see Isa. 38:4–6).

Think of the lessons Hezekiah learned of God's mercy and God's sovereignty during the end of his life (as well as God's care for the line of David and the city of Jerusalem). Think too of what it would be like to be told by God that you had exactly fifteen more years to live. But then think about the fact that God has indeed numbered your years just as exactly. Not one of us knows our number, but we can and must trust in the sovereign Ruler of the universe whom Scripture reveals.

At the start of a book that will take us into the territory of old age, how right to remember that our lives on this earth are like a fleeting dream or like grass that flourishes in the morning and withers in the evening (see Ps. 90:5–6)—all of which is divinely determined by the one who is God from everlasting to everlasting and who, according to his will, returns man to dust (see Ps. 90:1–3). We must approach this subject humbly, praying with the psalmist, "Teach us to number our days that we may get a heart of wisdom" (Ps. 90:12). Humility exalts not ourselves but our sovereign Lord God, acknowledging that we depend on him for every moment of life.

With this first great truth in place—the truth of our sovereign God who rules over every part of our human story, including our aging and death—we are ready to enter the rooms where our elderly loved ones live. We will go humbly indeed, knowing that we are seeing God's hand of judgment in a fallen world. We will certainly hate sin more, around us and in ourselves, as we witness its devastating effects. We will encounter the great enemy—death—as its hand reaches into various parts of weakening bodies. We will struggle against this enemy. And we will know that, even though we can help the weak, we cannot defeat death ourselves.

But as believers, we will know that Christ has done it. We know the big story. Jesus Christ the Son of God has already defeated this enemy. "It is finished," Jesus said from the cross as he paid the full price of death for our sin (John 19:30). And now the risen Christ reigns in heaven, until that day when he comes again to judge all and to make all things new. In the meantime, we live in this fallen world, trusting in God's sovereign redemptive plan, walking humbly to the end.

2

Responding with Humility

I need to go in. Mom is waiting. The biblical truths we celebrate must shape the experiences of our ordinary days, as we're looking to the end of not just the big story but—in the meantime—each little story. What I believe about my sovereign God must determine the way I interact with my mother today.

In the first chapter, we grappled with the first and foremost truth about aging: that our sovereign God rules over the process as he accomplishes his redemptive plan in human history. The aging process is linked to death, the enemy that rages in our world as a result of sin and according to the decree of our holy God. We looked at the big biblical story, in which we see that Christ on the cross defeated death—and we found our place in that story as believers, redeemed but still waiting for the final resolution.

We also said that the primary response to God's sovereignty over aging must be one of humility. This aging process is ordained by God as part of his story of redemption, and we must accept it from his hand, rather than deny it or complain about it or think we can fix it ourselves. We saw that King David's aged friend Barzillai understood this.

The missionary author Elisabeth Elliot famously and repeatedly said, "In acceptance lieth peace." Those words come from the final line of a poem by one whose life and work greatly influenced Elliot: the missionary Amy Carmichael.[1] If we read anything about the lives of these two strong godly women, both of whom faced immense suffering and loss in the midst of faithful service to the Lord, we quickly discover that the "acceptance" they taught was no passive giving up. It was humility in the act of receiving obediently what God put before them. Carmichael wrote that poem as she grieved the death of loved ones around her in the orphanage in India where she served, but she finally came to humbly accept the

> . . . breaking sorrow
> Which God tomorrow
> Will to His son explain.

How do we humbly accept the aging process from God's hand —as we deal with it in older generations, and, of course, as we prepare for it ourselves? First, our humble acceptance requires the honest acknowledgement that we cannot fix aging or make it go away.

Let's Speak Truth

The world around us is indeed good at pretending we can avoid old age. Those who have actually reached it know that we cannot.

1. The last line of the poem also serves as the title, "In Acceptance Lieth Peace," in *Mountain Breezes: The Collected Poems of Amy Carmichael* (Fort Washington, PA: Christian Literature Crusade, 1999), 293. Carmichael's biography is masterfully written by Elisabeth Elliot in *A Chance to Die: The Life and Legacy of Amy Carmichael* (Old Tappan, NJ: Fleming H. Revell, 1987). Elliot tells her own story of the martyrdom of her husband Jim in *Through Gates of Splendor* (New York: Harper, 1957). Elliot knew well the importance of this topic of caring for aging loved ones: she wrote of caring for her own elderly mother, who suffered dementia (even as she herself would, years later), in a long out-of-print book titled *Forget Me Not: Loving God's Aging Children* (Sisters, OR: Multnomah Publications, 1990).

A ninety-something-year-old person with ninety-something-year-old skin knows the truth about those well-marketed skin creams that help only a little and for a little while. The advertisers for the store Forever 21 have a limited marketing audience. One of the best gifts we can give our elderly loved ones is the gift of speaking truth with them about aging—that is, the truth that aging happens under God's sovereign rule, and that our role is to see aging and deal with it for what it is.

My mother's ophthalmologist is a good example of a truth-speaker. Mom has age-related macular degeneration; she's blind in one eye and sees a wee bit out of the other. Her doctor is a specialist in this disease. Perhaps because he knows so much, he is careful not to promise too much. In spite of a great deal of ongoing research into this kind of macular degeneration, there is as of yet no known cure, and my mother's doctor is straightforward about that fact. He does not offer any hope that she will get better.

He tests her eyes with amazing machines that map out the spread of the damaged areas, and the pictures look like lunar landscapes covered with shadows. He is happy that the shadows have not quite covered her eyes, and he says that, at this point, there is a good chance they will now stay where they are, so that she will not be completely blind. In the meantime, various supplements can help slow the process. He is interested in her case and her experience, and he takes time to listen to her descriptions of what things look like to her. He sends her to a specialist in eyeglasses and various aids for the vision-impaired. He is kind. Somehow my mother always leaves encouraged by him, even though he can't heal her disease and tells her so.

I appreciate this doctor and have learned from him about the goodness of honesty when dealing with aging. Now, honesty can perhaps go too far: I thought that was the case when, several years ago, my ailing father was sent to his medical association's "Heart Failure Clinic" for regular treatment . . . certainly they could have come up with a better name! And yet it was a true name—and it turned out to identify accurately what would take the life of my father within a few months.

I think it was around that time that my husband and I discussed with my parents what it means to create a "living will": a legal document that clarifies a person's preferences regarding medical treatment in the event that that person is unable to make his or her own decisions. Discussing this document together is good and helpful: not only does the living will protect a patient when the time comes to use it, but also the very process of creating it puts the realities of the end of life on the table as a necessary and profitable subject of conversation.[2]

A good doctor can be a helpful part of this discussion. There is a humility required of doctors, who are trained to fix our bodies but who, in the end, cannot fix everything. The best doctors have learned this humility; the worst will keep on fixing and promising to fix, well beyond the point when they actually can. We can learn much from the best doctors, the ones who have learned to face the ultimate reality of death and who are willing to help their patients live as well as possible in light of death.

This truth is clearly and movingly expressed in a book by surgeon Atul Gawande. Dr. Gawande tells the honest truth about his experiences with aging and dying patients, family, and friends. He discovered that his most meaningful interactions arose "from helping others deal with what medicine cannot do as well as what it can."[3] In his life and practice, Dr. Gawande was confronted with the basic human needs for honesty and mercy. In fact, in the book,

2. An excellent resource for thinking biblically and wisely about such matters is Bill Davis's *Departing in Peace: Biblical Decision-Making at the End of Life* (Phillipsburg, NJ: P&R Publishing, 2017).

3. Atul Gawande, *Being Mortal: Medicine and What Matters in the End* (New York: Picador, 2017), 260. I highly recommend this book full of Dr. Gawande's wise insights and moving stories.

he time and time again brushes close to what a Christian recognizes as gospel truth—sadly, that truth he does not know or tell.

The examples of my mother's eye doctor and Dr. Gawande show us the basic goodness of truth-telling when it comes to old age and death—among any and all people, Christians or not. Readers of this book will include those who care for believers and nonbelievers; the need for truth applies to us all.

For our unbelieving parents, the need for truth certainly spreads to the realm of the spiritual: if we ourselves are followers of Christ our Savior, then we know above all that our parents need to know the Savior. Their greatest need is faith in Jesus Christ, who died on the cross to save sinners. We can pray for the right moments to speak this truth to them clearly. We can bring believers into their presence who can share the love of Christ—and, if possible, take our loved ones into the fellowship and preaching of the church. We can share what we've been reading in the Bible, or give them books and recordings that communicate Christian truth, if they will read and listen.

Above all, we can pray (and ask others to pray with us) that, by God's Spirit, their hearts will be softened to believe the truth that gives them eternal life in Christ. *And* we can speak truth to them in *all* matters of life and death. The truth about aging and dying may help them confront the need for their salvation.

For those with believing parents, it is just as important to tell the truth. That we are Christians does not mean we should avoid talking about old age and dying and death; it means we can discuss these things without fear—and with hope, trusting in the plan of redemption ordained by our sovereign God. My parents' generation was and is not especially comfortable sharing their thoughts and feelings about such matters. Interestingly enough, however, if they have been Christians for a while, they probably know a lot of songs about heaven!

My father was a pastor, and my parents often sang duets in church together; the words of these old hymns of the church laid out a great avenue into discussions of all that a Christian looks forward to after death. My father was quite a reserved person, but when he used to lead the hymn sing for the elderly men and women in their retirement community, his face would beam. He would tell the gathered group, with their assorted walkers and wheelchairs and white heads, about the various hymn writers and their stories. He loved the many older hymns about the hope of heaven—they all did. "When we all get to heaven," they would sing out, "what a day of rejoicing that will be! When we all see Jesus, we'll sing and shout the victory."[4]

One way or another, we need to talk about aging and death, and we need to tell the truth. We are called humbly to accept what comes from God's sovereign hand. My mother's arthritis is almost surely not going to get better, and I'm not going to tell her that it will. We don't want to pretend. As we tell the truth, however, we can humbly call our aging loved ones to look outward, not inward.

Let's Lift Up Their Eyes

As we discussed in the first chapter of this book, the truth is bigger than one little part of the story. We are called humbly to accept the truth not just of sin and fallenness and death but of creation and redemption and the new creation to come. God's sovereign plan is large and beautiful. We need to tell the *whole* truth.

It's easy for me to talk about focusing on the big story. I took a lovely walk outside today, I interacted with neighbors, I watered my plants with a granddaughter, and I'm sitting here typing in my study with books scattered all around me. Tonight, I'm going to hear my grandchildren perform in a school orchestra concert.

My mother, however, isn't strong enough to go outside for a walk. She can't see to read or write, she has a sore hip, and she's

4. E. E. Hewitt, "Sing the Wondrous Love of Jesus," 1898.

worried about running out of her protein drinks before I get there next week. One of the threats of old age many observe is that, as our bodies develop all sorts of issues, our minds are drawn to focus obsessively on those issues. Our field of vision narrows as our bodies and their needs become consuming. The great sovereign Creator Redeemer God is often the last thing on our minds. As human beings at any age, we know this temptation: to become so focused on our bodies, our appearances, our health, and our comfort that we forget to look outside ourselves. But with the elderly these pressures are multiplied—more than we younger ones can imagine.

I have talked with numerous friends about the process of supervising medications for our aging parents, who often have many different pills to keep track of, both prescription medications and supplements. Perhaps you have handled those pillboxes with all the different compartments; perhaps you have tried to explain the compartments to an elderly person who can't see them very well, or who regularly turns them sideways, or upside down. Trying to manage this in a phone call is the worst possible scenario. I may have raised my voice multiple times while talking about pills over the phone, before Mom moved from her independent-living apartment to an assisted-living apartment in the retirement community where she lives—and where her pills are supervised and given to her.

It is amazing how consuming the medication process can be: as our bodies develop more and more needs, we depend more and more on various regularly timed pills. Not only do we make sure to take that blood pressure pill or that cholesterol pill, but we also seek out the latest supplements, hoping to get a clearer brain, or a better digestive system, or softer skin, and on and on—and all these pills become our daily manna, so to speak. We wouldn't dream of missing them (maybe more than we wouldn't dream of missing our Bible reading). Many of them we should not miss, of course. But how is it that they can take up so much of our time and energy and focus?

I like to wake up in the morning and think first about the Lord. But these days, I must first be sure to take a certain pill that requires time to digest before I can eat or drink anything else. I recall how an elderly friend who had severe arthritis described her morning routine: when she awoke, she spent about thirty minutes lying there, simply moving and stretching one part of her body, and then another, just so she could sit up and get out of bed. They humble us, these bodies.

Three Questions

How can we help our aged loved ones grapple with this growing and consuming focus on our needy bodies? How can we help lift their eyes outward and upward to the sovereign God who is directing a story much bigger than us and our small part?

Let me suggest three ways, by asking three basic questions.

First, *Is my loved one receiving adequate care?* I realize that question echoes with waves of implications and complications. Each situation is different. A person whose parent has Alzheimer's so often struggles to know just when that parent needs more daily help than their immediate family can give—or more help than a certain level of outside care can give. But there are some clear markers. Is my loved one in any evident danger without further care?

My mother came to the point where she was in danger of mismanaging her own medications; she needed daily help. (She also needed fewer of the supplements than she thought she did.) It became clear that she was in danger as well when she began to fall in the middle of the night; she needed to have someone right there to supervise and help, and that someone had to be capable of lifting and aiding her. I wish that my husband and I could have taken her into our home at some point. That is often a wonderful way to manage the later years, and it is the way many families and cultures have done it for centuries. In many cases, of course, those with elderly loved ones at home come to need more help. The basic question is, Does my loved one have adequate care? It can be humbling, both for caregivers and for those cared for, to admit that they need more help.

Adult children have been dealing with the changing and urgent needs of their parents for centuries. The Old Testament book of 1 Samuel tells us of David's care for his aged parents during the years when King Saul was chasing David through the wilderness to kill him—and David's family was in danger as well. For a time, David hid in the cave of Adullam, gathering to himself there about four hundred people, including those in distress, in debt, bitter in heart —*and* "his brothers and all his father's house" (1 Sam. 22:1). But David realized that he could not care adequately for his parents in the wilderness; it was probably too harsh a life for them. So, he took them to stay in Moab, the ancestral home of Ruth (the grandmother of Jesse, David's father). David went right to the king of Moab and arranged for the very best assisted-living accommodation:

> "Please let my father and my mother stay with you, till I know what God will do for me." And he left them with the king of Moab, and they stayed with him all the time that David was in the stronghold. (1 Sam. 22:3–4)

What a striking glimpse into how God's anointed king—through whose line would come the greater David, the King of Kings—cared for the poor and needy, including his own parents.

Once the need for adequate care is acknowledged and dealt with (for a time, at least . . . this question must be asked again and again), it is easier to work on the outward focus. These days, I don't spend nearly as much time with my mother discussing medications and other physical issues. Now that she has regular help and supervision, we can more often talk about other things, both on the phone and when I am with her. The most urgent physical needs are met, and I am thankful. She still measures out her days by the pills brought to her at various times, but she doesn't worry or obsess over them, and neither do I.

Here is one of the benefits of a higher level of care, when that level is possible: basic needs do not dominate our interaction with our parents. This means that I can and must give more time to discussing other things with my mother: what Sunday's sermon was about, how her good friend Peg is doing, how the grandchildren (great-grandchildren for her!) did in the school orchestra concert, and so on.

I must admit, sometimes it is easier just to manage the urgent physical needs. It takes patience and effort to discuss the sermon, or the music from the concert. In the end, of course, the question of whether my loved one is receiving adequate care must address my loved one's inner self—is she receiving adequate care of her whole being? Am *I* paying attention to the whole big story of God's redemption as I care for my mother, who is living out her chapters of that story? We will return to this.

Here is the second question we ought to ask: *Is my loved one receiving appropriate care?* With all the attention paid to needy bodies in the later years, it would be possible to keep doing things to them right up to the moment of their passing away. Doctors, and everybody else, love to fix things.

My dearly loved mother-in-law was diagnosed with breast cancer in her late eighties, in the course of a routine health check. Should she have undergone radiation or chemo? She had a doctor and family members who were happy for her to choose not to undergo cancer treatment—which might have extended her life but which certainly would have made it much more painful and, perhaps as a result, more inward-focused. As it turned out, the cancer seemed not to affect her during the several years she happily lived after the diagnosis, teaching piano lessons and enjoying friends and family until the very day she died of a heart attack at ninety-one. She was one of the most outward-focused people I've ever known, to the end. That was her story; other stories are different, and we must respect the differences in situations and decisions in such matters.

More and more, however, people seem to be embracing the wisdom of restraint when it comes to quick and aggressive medical intervention for people of advanced age (as in close to ninety years old). This is part of the thrust of Atul Gawande's *Being Mortal*, as he shares his experience of learning to discern when to rush to surgery and when to wait, depending on the human situation of the patient. It is a matter of deciding if and when the medical care is appropriate for the whole needs of the whole human being.

Most would agree that ongoing medicine and treatment to increase the stability of one's life (heart pressure meds, pain meds, physical therapy, and so on) are usually appropriate. Sometimes surgery is unavoidable—as in the case of my mother at age ninety-six, when her artificial hip of more than two decades basically fell apart, causing immobility and unbearable pain. Even then, though, should the old hip be replaced with a new one? Or should the disintegrating parts simply be replaced? How extensive a surgery should she be asked to handle? How long would the new or repaired hip need to hold?

I thank God for a wise and humble surgeon who did his best to put my mother through the smallest possible ordeal—although it was still a grueling process for her, leaving her much weakened. She did well trying to hold on to an outward focus during those weeks, although it took most of her energy to manage her basic bodily functions while wearing a hard plastic and steel body brace day and night in the skilled care unit. It seemed like a terrible humbling: to be regularly turned and lifted and cleaned and dressed by strong, younger nursing staff who usually try to understand but who really can't.

In discussing the first two questions that help us redirect the focus from needy bodies outward and upward, the third question has been unavoidable. Along with asking about adequate and appropriate care, we must keep asking about heart care. I'm using *heart* here in the biblical sense, meaning the very center of a person's invisible being, including thoughts and desires and emotions. It's the part of us that God sees and we can't: "Man looks on the outward appearance, but the LORD looks on the heart" (1 Sam. 16:7). The necessary third question is this: *Is my loved one receiving heart care?* Aside from all the consuming questions about physical and medical care, is my mother being loved and ministered to in a way that pulls her heart toward God?

We caretakers cannot do this all by ourselves; admitting this is part of the humility required to be good caretakers. We need other people, including the church body, to help care for our aging loved ones—particularly for their hearts. It is a shame that so many of the aged members of an average local congregation today are not known in the flesh by the younger members. Especially with the onset of COVID, older members disappeared. They were in the process of disappearing before that, with an increasing number of aging men and women living in nursing homes or retirement communities, often separated from families and local churches—and often not able to attend church gatherings regularly. Many continue to drive for a while, but at some point they don't, and then a church member must take the time and energy to go get an older person, help him or her into a car, perhaps load the walker or wheelchair, take him or her to church and watch over him or her there, and then make the return trip. I know some church members who do this, and I know both the bother and the blessing involved. But it happens less and less. May it happen more and more. May the elderly humbly receive help, and may members of Christ's body value and celebrate the humble service of all who bother themselves to give it.[5]

Pam Benton, mentor and teacher of many alongside her pastor husband, writes poignantly, "As Alzheimer's is stealing my

5. Bill Davis offers a helpful discussion of Christians' need to "embrace the Bible's valuing of the dependent and the caregivers" in *Departing in Peace*, 85–86.

husband's memory and his needs grow greater and my strength weakens, the body of Christ grows more precious. Friends take him to Bible study, hiking, and out to lunch and breakfast, and they are available to help me. As they come alongside Wilson and me, I am enabled to help other women flourish."[6]

For housebound aging loved ones, we can visit, and we can invite others to visit. We can make sure their minds receive stimulation, through human interaction and through well-chosen books or recordings. I find that biographies, especially missionary biographies, are often encouraging for an older person; there is great benefit in getting out of my own little life and into the life story of another in a different time and place. In the case of a person with impaired eyesight like my mom, recordings of some kind are especially important. My mother never learned to manage technology; she left it to Dad, and now she is in many ways unable to handle it, as she cannot discern words or figures on screens. For several years, she enjoyed listening to books on CDs; now she most often listens to a small audio Bible that she has painstakingly learned to charge and manage. I'm grateful for that Bible, and so is she.

Above all, we need to take in the very Word of God, which reminds us over and over of the real story, the big story, written by God's sovereign hand from beginning to end. The Bible tells us the truth, the whole truth. I loved it when, the other day, my mother called me and said, "Well, I just listened to the whole book of Romans, and I want to ask you about those chapters that talk about Jacob and Esau . . ."

And then there is television—which we all know can be like a pacifier, no matter our age. Living with the TV on, constantly

6. Sharon W. Betters and Susan Hunt, *Aging with Grace: Flourishing in an Anti-Aging Culture* (Wheaton, IL: Crossway, 2021), Kindle. The authors share many testimonies of both aging ones and caregivers who have found strength from generous fellow believers.

numbing our brains, is a fierce temptation for older men and women who spend a lot of time sitting or reclining, often alone. My mom, whose hearing has declined as well, has a pair of what I call her rabbit ears, a little headset she wears that gives her the TV audio directly. When she's wearing her headset she sort of disappears, most often into the world of cable news. But she knows to come out regularly.

It's not a bad thing for Mom to keep track of what's going on in the larger world. (And it's a wonderful thing for her to have television access to the various chapel and vesper services held there in her retirement community.) We just don't want those TV voices to numb our loved ones' hearts, so that they lose the habit of looking outward and upward, to the real story of what God is doing in this world—and in us.

We have to be there, in the flesh, to ask these questions. We need to look old age in the face—literally. To judge adequate care, and appropriate care, and heart care, we do well, if at all possible, to spend extended time in the bodily presence of our aging loved ones. We need to hear their voices, watch them get up from a chair, see how much they eat and with what kind of appetite, pray with them, ask them questions, and look in their eyes as they talk.

This kind of time spent, in little things and little spaces, may make us caregivers feel that we've been pulled out of the big story's main action. In fact, strangely enough, we've been pulled in to the center. To live in God's big story is to live in human bodies that we must deal with, from beginning to end. We make our way through God's sovereign plan of redemption as embodied creatures; he made us this way. The journey becomes more and more humbling as bodies become more and more needy with age. But we have a remarkable opportunity to help our aging loved ones humbly accept what God brings—and to learn to do the same ourselves.

After all, God came down to us in a body. He doesn't just sit up there above the circle of the earth, watching us grasshoppers from a distance as he stretches out the heavens and directs the course of human history. The Son of God came down. That's the turning point of the big story. And that turning point shapes all our little stories as well. We little creatures make our appearance, grow, and then weaken and die. But the sovereign God sees us all, always. He planned salvation for us. He came himself to save us. He is coming again. We can look to him, humbly, in faith, to the end.

3

God Calls Us to Honor Our Elders

The first big biblical truth we encountered is that aging occurs under God's sovereign rule. The second is that God calls us to honor our elders. We find this call repeatedly throughout the Scriptures: elders (both parents and older people in general) are to be respected and honored in the sovereign God's generational order.

Generations: God's Idea, for His Glory

The Bible is clear that God created human beings to live in generations; we should notice this, and we might well wonder why. Even before the fall, God created Adam and Eve and told them to "be fruitful and multiply and fill the earth" (Gen. 1:28). We do not know what aging human beings would have been like without the entrance of sin and death into the story, but we do know that, from the beginning, humans were created to live generation after generation, as babies are born, grow up, and produce more babies, and on and on!

Our Creator designed the human race, then, to be ordered according to parents and children, older and younger, again and again—as we often trace in family trees. Each of us is a branch of a tree, whether we can trace it or not. The book of Genesis, which tells us our shared human beginnings, can be divided into clear sections that begin with the heading (or a slight variant of the heading) "These are the generations of . . ." (2:4; 5:1; 6:9; 10:1; 11:10, 27; 25:12, 19; 36:1, 9; 37:2).

Through this principle of generations, which is evidenced in all living creatures, God must have wanted to keep showing his own glorious generative power, as it spreads and multiplies through time and place. All life comes from our God in heaven, who has life in himself; all life apart from him is derived life, and that life is meant to grow and show his glory throughout the earth. Among human beings created in God's image, this generative power points us to our Creator, who allows and enables us created beings to participate in his plan to multiply human life generation by generation —reflecting his glory over and over again.

In a myriad of ways, we humans reflect the three-personed God who made us; we are created to share in the mysterious eternal fellowship and unity of Father, Son, and Holy Spirit. The original blueprint of Father and Son is in the very being of God; how amazing that, in God's redemptive plan, it is through God's *Son* that we fallen creatures enter into fellowship with him, the first and ultimate Father. For good reason the apostle Paul says that he bows his knees "before the Father, from whom every family in heaven and on earth is named" (Eph. 3:14–15).

The biblical principle of respecting our parents and our elders in general, then, rests in the larger principle that generations themselves point us back to God, who is both the origin and the Redeemer of all our human generations. If there is a deep reason for the decline of respect for elders in recent generations of the Western world, that reason must be the decline of belief in God, the God revealed in the pages of Scripture from the beginning.

Other parts of the world seem to do better in respecting parents and elders. I have spent much time in Asia, where it is easy to notice the deference given to elderly people—even in such little matters as listening respectfully to them, making sure they are seated well, and so forth. Traditions (and traditions rooted in various religious systems) often govern such practices. Even so, one wonders whether, at some deep level, these other cultures have held on by common grace to an important part of our reflection of the image of God.

Respecting parents and elders is not just good manners. According to the Bible, such respect is rooted in God's creation of us to honor him. In this chapter and the next, we will consider not just how to be polite, but rather how we can join a rhythm of relationships that reflects and pleases the God of the universe. It's not a little thing but a big thing—this truth that God calls human beings to honor our elders. And it's not an abstract truth but a personal truth—this truth that honoring our elders involves our relationship with the Lord God. Many a time, when I grow tired of this seemingly long process of honoring, it strengthens my heart and lifts my spirit to know that I am doing this for the glory of the Father God I love, enabled by his very presence within me through his Spirit.

A Story of Generations

In Scripture, the call to honor elders begins with the call to honor parents. After all, the human race started out with a pair of parents. The story of Cain and Abel in Genesis 4 is bookended by Adam "knowing" his wife and bearing sons—first Cain (see 4:1) and then, after Cain murders his brother, Seth (see 4:25). Genesis 5 then traces Seth's line up until Noah, who fathered three sons from whom the whole human race grew after the flood. The Bible's story is indeed one of generations.

In the narrative of the generations after Noah, we immediately see the importance of children's respect for parents. Consider, for example, that strange little post-flood episode in which Noah "became drunk and lay uncovered in his tent" (9:21). The story focuses less on the bad behavior of Noah and more on the response of his sons: "Ham, the father of Canaan," looked on his father's nakedness and told his brothers all about it (v. 22), whereas Shem and Japheth took a covering, walked into the tent backward so they could not see their naked father, and covered him. When Noah woke up and learned what had happened, he spoke a curse on Canaan, the son of Ham, but he spoke a blessing on the families of Shem and Japheth. And we learn in the following chapters that from Shem's line would come the line of Abraham.

No narrative commentary on this scene helps us interpret it, but the horror seems to lie in Ham's exposure, not just to himself but to others, of his father's folly and vulnerability. It seems likely that he scorned or mocked his father, although we don't know for sure. His father is the one God had chosen to build the ark that saved them and the representative with whom God had established his covenant with the sign of a rainbow in the sky. In this very next scene, then, poor drunk naked father Noah should still be respected. The actions of the other two sons make this clear, as does Noah's curse on Canaan.

But how interesting that the storyline turns on the disrespect of a son for his father. Ham's line developed into the Canaanites, who turned from God to idols and who were severely judged by God when their land was given to the Israelites during Joshua's time. The principle of children honoring parents was, of course, explicitly articulated in the law given to the ones who would inhabitant that land and was directly related to their longevity there: as the fifth commandment states, "Honor your father and your mother, that your days may be long in the land that the Lord your God is giving you" (Ex. 20:12).

The first section of the Ten Commandments (commandments one through four) is all about honoring God; the second section is about honoring those around us and focuses immediately on honoring *parents*. This fifth commandment is reiterated throughout the books of the Law. For example, in Leviticus 19:2–3, the first words to follow the monumental command "You shall be holy, for I the LORD your God am holy" are these: "Every one of you shall revere his mother and his father."

The principle then broadens from honoring parents to honoring elders in general. Later in that same chapter of Leviticus, as God's words to Moses continue, comes a verse I've always considered hugely instructive, not only because of its initial command but also because of the one attached to it. These commands come together: "You shall stand up before the gray head and honor the face of an old man, and you shall fear your God: I am the LORD" (Lev. 19:32). Honoring the elderly and fearing God: they go together.

In the Song of Moses, part of the prophet's final words inspired by God to give to Israel, a similar connection appears: Moses turns the people first to the Lord their "father" and then to their earthly fathers. After a reproach for their sin, Moses writes these powerful words:

> Do you thus repay the LORD,
>   you foolish and senseless people?
> Is not he your father, who created you,
>   who made you and established you?
> Remember the days of old;
>   consider the years of many generations;
> ask your father, and he will show you,
>   your elders, and they will tell you. (Deut. 32:6–7)

The book of Proverbs offers a live portrayal of fathers and mothers instructing the next generation: the first nine chapters include a series of calls to wisdom from a father to a son. Yes, the mother is there and is often mentioned—and indeed, we can understand that the wisdom offered is applicable to daughters as well as sons! The clear principle is that elders are to be respected and heeded by the younger generation. "Listen to your father who gave you life," we read, "and do not despise your mother when she is old" (Prov. 23:22). Along with the commands come remarkably vivid warnings:

> The eye that mocks a father
> and scorns to obey a mother
> will be picked out by the ravens of the valley
> and eaten by the vultures. (Prov. 30:17)

Lack of honor for elders inevitably comes with sin and upheaval. Lamentations 5 offers a great example on a large scale: the prophetic writer laments the fall of Jerusalem, where now princes are killed, women are raped, and "no respect is shown to the elders" (Lam. 5:12).

These representative verses reveal the Bible's loud, almost overwhelming call to respect our elders—and to do so as part of our reverence for the Lord God who made us. Perhaps too often children hear only the fifth commandment, without putting that commandment in the context of the whole biblical story from Genesis onward. The Ten Commandments come in a context, as part of the big story of a sovereign Creator God who calls out and delivers his people and then graciously reveals himself to them, guiding them as a father guides his child. We will do well to hear and to pass on the commandments, including the fifth, as part of the whole counsel of God our heavenly Father.

Making Return

The call to honor our elders does not depend on the honorability of our elders. The story of Noah and his sons offers an instructive example. Perhaps Proverbs 23:22 tells us not to despise our mothers when they are old because mothers (and fathers) sometimes become foolish in their old age—sometimes in ways they can help, and sometimes in ways they cannot (we'll come back to this). In that same proverb, fathers are to be listened to *because they gave us life*. We are to care respectfully for the generation before us, who brought us into this world. The apostle Paul affirms this principle as he instructs the children and grandchildren of widows to provide godly support first for their own household "and to make some return to their parents, for this is pleasing in the sight of God" (1 Tim. 5:4).

I love that phrase "make some return to their parents." It's not just acceptable but good to think of caring for our parents as giving back to them in the ways they gave to us, often very physical ways. It's not as if we could ever make full return—but we can make some. Our parents gave us life: that is the ultimate good they did us. They conceived, carried, and delivered us into this world. They took care of us or made sure we were cared for when we were most needy—that is, most of them did. We all know there are exceptions, sorrowful exceptions that break our hearts. But the God-given instinct of most parents, by his grace, is to feed and clothe and watch over children as they grow from infancy.

We were all demanding from the start, every one of us human beings. Funny that we don't remember it. We often smelled bad. Our naked little bodies looked so helpless. We cried loudly. We couldn't be reasoned with. We disturbed our parents' schedules and sleep. We quickly grew into time-consuming toddlers. We needed companionship and comfort and words . . . many kinds of help. It makes sense that, at the other end of life, we grown-up children should "make some return" to our parents, perhaps in these very ways. By God's grace, let us make good return.

Of course, the ultimate help a child needs, and our parents need—and even we need right now—is to be turned to the Father who made us. Perhaps the hugest benefit of caring for aging parents is that, in doing so, we may be turned to our first parent, our Father in heaven who gave us life and who gives us eternal life with him through his Son. As our earthly parents weaken, we look to the unchanging and perfectly loving heavenly Father. Indeed, even as we care for them, the humbling realization of what we were all like as cared-for infants gives us just a glimpse of how our God sees us and lovingly cares for us in our sin and our unending need.

We cannot make any return to our heavenly Father by ourselves, dirtied by sin and needy as we are. Only through his Son can we come to him. Only dressed in Christ's righteousness can we serve him. And one of the ways we do this is by honoring our parents. The New Testament calls children to obey their parents "in the Lord" (Eph. 6:1); such obedience "pleases the Lord" (Col. 3:20). From start to finish, honoring our parents is ultimately all about honoring our Maker and Redeemer. To reject this command is to turn away from God. If we are uncomfortable making that point, it helps that the apostle Paul does so in the strongest possible terms: "But if anyone does not provide for his relatives, and especially for members of his household, he has denied the faith and is worse than an unbeliever" (1 Tim. 5:8).

Aging in the Church Family

Since we've moved to the New Testament, let's think a bit more about how it talks about older people in the church. Paul's commands come to members of church bodies, followers together of the Lord Jesus Christ. That is where God's people live now, in our part of the biblical story: not in the nation of Israel led by prophets, priests, and kings but in the church, the body of Christ for whom the final Prophet, Priest, and King came and died and rose again.

All the Old Testament principles of honoring parents and elders carry on into the New, but today we believers have a marvelous opportunity to live out those principles in the fellowship of the church, with the full revelation of God's completed Word and with the power of the indwelling Spirit of the risen Christ. For a Christian, this perspective makes all the difference as we care for our elderly loved ones: we do this work not alone but surrounded by brothers and sisters in Christ who hold up our arms in all kinds of ways.

Although the elderly do not earn the honor and respect that is their due, the Bible makes it clear that the wisdom and maturity that often accompany old age are desirable blessings, fitting gifts God uses to pass on his truth to the next generations. Paul's instructions to Titus concerning the church family include specific directions for "older men" and "older women" (see Titus 2:2–3). The qualities Paul lists are ones we can pray for and help cultivate, as well as learn from, in our parents and in the older members of our churches, and they are clearly qualities we can aim to develop in ourselves as we get older.

Many of my friends and I have discussed the irony of God's timing in all this: we who care for elderly parents are often just approaching the category of "old" ourselves! This is inconvenient, for our own bones and joints might well ache as we lift our parent's wheelchair in and out of the car. The timing is actually perfect, however, for we are blessed as if with a loud alarm: *Old age is coming! Do you see it? Are you aiming and praying in the right direction?*

Paul is clear about this direction:

> Older men are to be sober-minded, dignified, self-controlled, sound in faith, in love, and in steadfastness. Older women likewise are to be reverent in behavior, not slanderers or slaves to much wine. They are to teach what is good, and so train the young women to love their husbands and children, to be self-controlled, pure, working at home, kind, and submissive to their own husbands, that the word of God may not be reviled. (Titus 2:2–5)

It would take more books than this to unpack the substance of these verses. They call for much prayerful meditation. They also, of course, have elicited much argument. But it helps to start with prayerful meditation, and *humble* meditation: what challenging qualities of older men and women these are! The theme of self-control (sobriety, dignity, reverence, careful speech) speaks to any age—but perhaps especially to older ones, who may not feel they have as much to gain or prove and who may become less restrained in their actions and words as they age.

At the very least, older people are called to press on in the disciplines of a faithful life. They are to be mature in their faith: for men to be "sound in faith, in love, and in steadfastness," and for women to "teach what is good," implies that both groups will have studied the Scriptures, learned good doctrine, and cultivated an ability to share humbly and effectively the truths they have learned and lived.

Out of such a store of qualities comes the wisdom of old age. Such qualities enable the father and mother in Proverbs to call the next generation to wisdom. God means for this flow of wisdom to be passed on from older to younger; what a great responsibility to be part of that flow, both in the receiving and in the giving. The Israelites repeatedly rejected that responsibility, perhaps most dramatically right after they finally settled in the promised land under the godly leadership of Joshua, with all sorts of ceremonies and vows to remember and follow God's word. Early on in the book of Judges, however, we read these sad words: "And there arose another generation after them who did not know the Lord or the work that he had done for Israel" (Judg. 2:10). The context of Israel's history makes these words of the psalmist even more urgent:

> I will utter dark sayings from of old,
> things that we have heard and known,
> that our fathers have told us.
> We will not hide them from their children,
> but tell to the coming generation
> the glorious deeds of the Lord, and his might,
> and the wonders that he has done. (Ps. 78:2–4)

This is the ideal: faithfully passing on God's truth to the next generation. Our aging loved ones—and we ourselves—will often fall far from it. But it is important to hold the ideal in our thoughts and prayers. As we have seen, Paul sets forth the qualities older men and women in the church should seek in order to attain this ideal. By the power of the Spirit and the Word, these qualities do grow and flourish among God's people, as his truth is lived out generation by generation. We are meant to honor our elders, to learn from them, and to become "older" ones who pass on the faith.

Anna the prophetess is one of my favorite old people in the Bible. Luke tells us she was "advanced in years," a faithful widow who "did not depart from the temple, worshiping with fasting and prayer night and day" (Luke 2:36, 37). I imagine her face was wrinkled and welcoming. I imagine a lot of younger people knew her, cared for her, and learned from her. Anna got to meet Jesus, the promised Messiah she waited for so steadfastly. When Joseph and Mary brought the child Jesus to the temple for the required sacrifices, both the righteous old man Simeon and the faithful old widow Anna recognized who he was. Simeon offered a glorious blessing, and Anna "began to give thanks to God and to speak of him to all who were waiting for the redemption of Jerusalem" (2:38). Anna knew him, Anna gave thanks for him, and Anna told others about him. The Scriptures call us to see and learn from beautiful Anna.

We who live as part of the church have surely seen good real-life examples—perhaps in our parents and perhaps in other older, faithful people—who have taught us and shown us what is good in God's sight. There is always something to learn from an older person, even the most imperfect one. If we take time to listen well and humbly, we will learn. As a young teen, I had a faithful, older Sunday school teacher who showed me what it looked like to study and love God's Word; I can still see her holding her marked-up Bible and instructing us from it. In recent years, I have benefitted from knowing my mother's friends, many of whom know the Lord like she does and bear testimony to "the glorious deeds of the LORD" and "the wonders that he has done" (Ps. 78:4).

There is a growing host of elderly people within the church and outside the church these days—a whole host to honor, in a host of ways. They can show us much of God's grace, and we can show them the same. For the ones who do not know the Lord Jesus Christ, our honor and service may be used by God to help open paths of faith in their hearts.

It is easy to find ways of excusing ourselves from this call to honor the elderly. We younger people are busy—even busy serving the Lord. Jesus got after the Pharisees for manufacturing such excuses:

> And he said to them, "You have a fine way of rejecting the commandment of God in order to establish your tradition! For Moses said, 'Honor your father and your mother'; and, 'Whoever reviles father or mother must surely die.' But you say, 'If a man tells his father or his mother, "Whatever you would have gained from me is Corban"' (that is, given to God)—then you no longer permit him to do anything for his father or mother, thus making void the word of God by your tradition that you have handed down. And many such things you do." (Mark 7:9–13)

The Pharisees had established a tradition through which funds that should have been used to care for one's parents could be labeled "Corban" (meaning "dedicated to God") and thereby rechanneled to the temple coffers. Thus, church leaders were getting rich at the expense of parents, who were being neglected. How telling that Jesus chose this example to challenge the Pharisees' hypocritical self-righteousness: one of the most basic requirements of the law, honoring father and mother, was being discarded with a seemingly holy excuse.

I do not offer this example to deepen the guilt of those who are doing their best to care for their parents but aching that they can never do it as well as they would like, especially given the other commitments they have made to serve the Lord. We can never do this perfectly. In my international travel, I have often spoken with those serving in missions who are sorrowing that they cannot spend more time with their aging parents. Each situation is unique; we cannot judge any one of them from the outside. I have met countless missionaries who are doing their utmost to assure the best care for their parents, often through other family members who are able to be more closely involved, and often through more travel and irregular schedules than they might otherwise have chosen, in order to be involved enough themselves. I have also met many elderly parents who delight to pray for their children who are serving the Lord far away; some parents make it easier, and some do make it harder.

Jesus's point is that it is reprehensible to try to make ourselves look righteous while we are disregarding God's Word, often aiming for our own comfort. That point speaks to adult children who think they are too busy, too important, or even too offended to heed the command to honor our parents. This command is God's Word to us, and we must seek with all our hearts to hear and obey. In the next chapter, we will aim to get at what this looks like in practice.

In his providence, God ordered our human existence by generations, older and younger, again and again until Jesus returns. As we faithfully play our part within the flow of generations, honoring the ones before us, we honor our heavenly Father who sent us his Son.

4

Responding with Respect

The second big biblical truth looms large: God calls us to honor our elders and thus to honor him. And now we have to live it out. As I enter my mother's room in her assisted-living community, everything depends on the bent of my heart to honor her. The bent of my heart, of course, depends on God's grace at work in me—perhaps the best advice for caretakers of the elderly is to read the Bible, pray every day, and go to church regularly!

I write that with a smile, but I know it is profoundly true. It might be that simple. Only by God's grace at work in my heart can I come with his eyes and his love for this unique human being he has created. It is the ordinary means of grace (Word, prayer, the fellowship of the saints) that equip any of us to respond to our aging loved ones with the kind of respect they are due.

Respecting in a World of Disrespect

On my own, I might begrudge my time and effort. I might put on a display of respect that is not true respect. On my own, I might be tempted to belittle my aging parent who suffers decline, physical or mental. To be sure, the culture around us increasingly urges on such attitudes. If you are old enough to remember TV shows like *Father Knows Best* or *Leave It to Beaver*, you recall the moms and dads in those domestic comedies as stereotypical, yes, but also as generally wise and good. But move ahead to a popular show like *The Simpsons*: here, as I recall reading, it's the kids who are the "wise guys"—both parents are foolish in their own way. *Parents are stupid*, many kids have been learning (and many parents have been learning as well).

The implications of these evolving attitudes spread into many areas of life, especially child-rearing, in which the will and the immediate happiness of each child now seem to rule over all, including parents. But that is another book. This book treats the long-term effects of such attitudes, as more and more adult children regard their aged parents with the same disrespect that is being fostered in young children from an early age.

I should stop and say that this is one area in which Christians increasingly stand out as different. Christians in general aim to follow the Scriptures in raising their children to know the Lord and obey him—and to obey their parents in the Lord. Christians in general also understand that the call to honor our parents and elders lasts a lifetime.

This honoring will not stand, however, without careful effort and biblical teaching that confronts head-on the wrongful attitudes and assumptions of the world around us. The rewards of such effort and teaching will be great. As we in the church aim to live out God's plan for biological families and church families, we not only honor our God but also have a huge opportunity to show his goodness to the world around us. Nowhere is that more important and urgent than in our care for the increasing numbers of aging ones among us.

How do we carry out this biblical call to honor our elders? What does this look like in practice? It looks like respect. In what follows, I will suggest three ways of living out this call to honor our aging loved ones: through patiently respecting their personhood, carefully respecting their dignity, and consistently respecting their work. These kinds of respect do not always come naturally or easily—and, again, we will never honor our elders perfectly. Even as the Lord graciously enables us to practice respect, he graciously forgives all our failures for the sake of Christ our Savior.

Patiently Respect Personhood

The first way in which we can live out the call to honor our elders is through *patiently respecting their personhood*.

Whom do I see when I enter Mom's room? Do I see a frail elderly body? Do I see the anxious face that rushes to deliver the deluge of tasks that need doing, the errands, the fix-it needs, the mail she couldn't read? Do I see the lovely white hair? Do I see a carrier of memories and experiences I do not know? Do I see a body that grew up from youth, that ran, that drove cars, that loved, that worked hard? Do I see the unique treasure of a human being created in God's image? Do I stop and see this person? Do I remember that I am looking not merely at a part of my life but at the end of a separate, God-ordained life? Do I try to see this life with God's eyes?

It takes patience to step back and see. It takes patience to respect this person in front of me. One major obstacle to proper respect is our impatience with various tendencies that often emerge in an aging person. We caregivers see these tendencies in ourselves, if we're honest—and perhaps that makes us even more frustrated (secretly fearful?) when we see them in our elders.

There's first and foremost the tendency to forget things, whether names or conversations or important numbers . . . and on and on. When an elderly person forgets or confuses something, especially something that, to us, seems clear or unforgettable or necessary, it can be hard not to pounce, authoritatively correct, and perhaps even reproach—like we might do to a child. Maybe we're just trying to get the bills paid, and our parent's forgetfulness is seriously slowing down the process. Where did she put that credit card, or to whom did she give it to do an errand for her? What did she tell that person on the phone? Who is the "he" she just started talking about without saying a name because she can't bring it to mind?

In most cases, forgetfulness is not something that aging people can help. Sometimes they could be more careful, and we can urge them in that direction. But as brains age, people just tend to become more forgetful. It is good for us younger ones to acknowledge this and to *intend* to be patient in the face of it. I regularly remind myself not to say to my mother, "You know I already told you that"—especially if she claims that I never did tell her that! There is no point in trying to be right. It constantly amazes me how my sinful self can be pricked into wanting to win a petty little argument with someone who is over ninety years old. The very worst is when it turns out that *I'm* "misremembering," to use one of my friend's favorite words. And that, of course, happens not uncommonly—at which point I try to thank God for humbling me.

The particular part of the story in which we caregivers get to participate is not all about us; it's about us honoring our parents. To the end, they are the ones who gave us life. They are God's loved ones who lived full lives with many roles and responsibilities about which we have no clue. To honor them is to lift them up. That means we put ourselves below them. We often hear or say that, later in life, roles get reversed: children become more like the parents, and the parents become more like children, needing oversight and help with many things. There is much truth to that. But there is a limit to that truth. Our parents are not called to obey us. We children are always the children, no matter how needy or helpless our parents become. The command to honor them never points anywhere but to us as children, who must respect those who never cease to be our parents, no matter what.

It is a never-ending wonder to me that, as Jesus was suffering on the cross, bearing the sins of the world, he gave thought to his mother (see John 19:26–27). In the midst of accomplishing his Father's eternal plan of redemption, he saw his mother standing by his cross, and he took thought for her needs. He respected and honored her. We should not be purely sentimental about this story. Jesus was in fact obeying God's law perfectly to the very end—and that law includes the fifth commandment. This part of the crucifixion story is not a small, incidental moment; it is one crucial part of Jesus's completely faithful obedience to his heavenly Father.

Here is the perfect sacrifice in action. At this point, Jesus's mother was probably widowed and needy, and Jesus made provision for her even as he was in the agonizing throes of making provision for the salvation of all God's people. Just as David made provision for his aged parents amid his own distress back in 1 Samuel 22, so this greater David made provision for his mother. He entrusted her to John, "the disciple whom he loved" (John 19:26). He knew that John would faithfully care for her in his absence. The very Son of God helps show us how to honor and respect our parents to the end.

Loved Ones with Dementia

At this point, let me stop and address the situation of so many who have elderly loved ones with various forms of dementia—the most extreme and tragic form of forgetting. I have had to depend on friends, many friends, for glimpses into what it's like to see a loved one slipping away mentally. My sister had a brain disease that quickly took away her ability to function, but that was a different experience from the kinds of dementia, such as Alzheimer's, that gradually erase the memory and other functions of the brain, especially in aging people.

How does the adult child of a parent with Alzheimer's respect the personhood of one who is losing control of memory and thoughts? My friends with experience in this area give me no easy answers, only the consistent encouragement to continue treasuring, spending time with, and praying for our loved one. One great avenue of help is to keep listening to and learning from others (whether live or through writing) who have experienced and/or researched the best ways to relate to dementia sufferers.

One of my good friends in our church congregation watched Alzheimer's develop and gradually take over her mother, who now lives close by in an assisted-living facility where my friend can be with her often and oversee her care. (In institutional situations, including hospitals, elderly people in any physical or mental condition need a friend or a loved one to oversee their care actively, especially today, when medical workers and aides are difficult to find and keep.)

My friend described to me her many efforts to talk with her mother about what was happening during early stages of the disease, but she discovered that her mother was not able to understand. Doctors later diagnosed her mother with a condition called *anosognosia*, which is an impaired ability to grasp one's own mental illness. It was important for my friend to learn about this kind of impairment—hard as it was to accept. How challenging for a child not to be able to process any of the loss with her parent who is undergoing it . . . it's like seeing that parent walk away into the distance without being able to say goodbye. As the separation happens, caregivers learn not to overexplain or correct or contradict; sufferers of dementia can be stubborn and utterly convinced of their unreality.

My friend wrote, "I have realized that so much of her stubbornness in not listening to me is her attempt to hold on to her dignity as a person. It's very easy to become frustrated with someone who has dementia/Alzheimer's, and I have come to understand that she can't control what she is going through, and my job is to love her and support her and give her respect as a person." What a wise daughter, my friend. Even while experiencing the greatest disconnect with the person of her mother, she is learning more and more to respect her mother's most basic personhood. What differentiates us human beings from the animals is that we are persons made in the image of God. That is the substance of our personhood, and it can never be taken away.

My friend described the process of packing up her mother's belongings as they moved her into the memory unit of her retirement community. Opening one box, she found her mother's prayer journals. Her mother has known the Lord for many years, and this was the sweetest reminder of what was still true, though presently invisible. "I realized that those journals were evidence of my mother's trust in Christ," my friend wrote, "and ultimately that is the only thing that truly matters in life and death."

I have no medical research to support my firm belief that we should speak and sing and read truth and beauty into the ears of those who apparently cannot understand any of it—but family members of unresponsive loved ones consistently share this belief. Visiting my sister in the final stages of her brain disease, it was impossible to tell how much she understood of what was said to her—but I loved singing some old hymns and reading the Bible and talking about heaven there by her bed. Her family and friends faithfully carried on the day-by-day ministry to her in this very way.

Who knows how much truth and beauty and love seeps down into the depths of such a person's heart and mind and soul? The Holy Spirit is like the wind that blows where it wills, working in ways we cannot see. Angels are watching and ministering. There is always more to the story than our eyes can take in.

Many who have cared for aging loved ones with dementia emphasize that we must not take personally their seeming disregard, or even unkindness, toward us who love them so much. They cannot control what is happening to them; we should not hold them responsible for hurting us—and we need to remind ourselves of this often.

This principle applies to more situations than just dementia, for elderly people in general often lose some of the self-control they practiced in their younger days. Many of my fellow caregivers of the elderly have noticed this movement toward less control, less restraint. It is understandable: as people age and gradually lose control over things they have always controlled (schedules, houses, cars, food, bladders!), along with all that loss comes a corresponding letting loose of emotions and words. These moments can seem like childhood tantrums sometimes, but they're even more complicated. We children are not here to discipline our parents or to teach them how to behave; we are here to love and help them while honoring and respecting them as our parents.

For several days after one major surgery, my mother experienced a severe response to the anesthesia, a temporary brain disorder called *post-operative delirium*. This is a condition of which caregivers should be aware, as it is apparently common in seniors. I had no prior knowledge of it and was completely unprepared for my mother's anger, suspicion, and inability to recognize me. She imagined that all the people around her were trying to hurt her. It did not help, of course, that my mother is almost blind, and, after staying in one hospital room after another, she became totally disoriented. (She now remembers some of this experience and does talk about it.)

I vividly remember calling my husband on the first night, in shock, trying to digest how my mother had treated me and others. It was painful, and I felt helpless. But I quickly learned what was happening and understood that I could not take this personally: my mother's brain was confused by the anesthesia and the physical trauma she had undergone. Her "real self" was hiding in there somewhere. It was a joy to watch over her and to see that self reemerge. How hard it is for those who never get to see that "real self" again in this life. How important for us to remind ourselves that it is still there, hidden away, known and seen by a sovereign and loving God.

Carefully Respect Dignity

The second way in which we can live out the call to honor our elders is through *carefully respecting their dignity.* This second point involves a practical working-out of the first point (*patiently respecting their personhood*), and it calls for active effort not to put down but to lift up our loved ones in the eyes of others, including ourselves.

Getting old involves so much of what feels like indignity—that is, being treated as foolish, or being shamed in some way. It is easy to trespass on the dignity of my mother, for example, when I talk with medical professionals about her in her presence, too often assuming that she cannot understand or that she doesn't mind having her insides laid out and discussed right in front of her. It is true that often she cannot understand, partly because the conversation goes too fast for her to hear and follow; she is simply left behind. At such times, how important it is to stop, to speak slowly and carefully, to address questions, and to include her in the conversation as much as possible.

Careful conversations are crucial. How many adult children have struggled to talk with their parents about selling a house and moving to a safer place, or about ending a driving career that has become risky due to poor eyesight and slow responses? Taking time for more than one conversation, prayer, patient discussion, more prayer, consultation with wider family and friends, and even more prayer are all helpful steps in the process. Respecting our parent's or parents' dignity throughout all these steps never ceases to be of prime importance, as we encourage their questions and thoughts and as we wait (sometimes longer than we would like) for them to come round to what we consider the wise decision.

Surely there are times when the children must step in and impose a decision for the safety of their parent—particularly in situations where the instability or ill health of the parent makes good judgment impossible. On the other hand, I know of many situations in which aging parents have made these sorts of decisions on their own, before their children or friends even broached the subject. Let us watch and learn, Lord; let us watch and learn.

In matters both large and small, it is good for us caregivers to think of ourselves as protectors of our elders' dignity. When our aging loved ones experience incontinence, for example, we can be careful not to speak of these issues carelessly or publicly. My mother is actually quite relaxed about these matters; it helps that she has friends who are experiencing many of the same problems—and they laugh and joke together about their various pads and pills and walkers and protein drinks. It is important for them to have a safe place to talk about such things, and to have other safe places where such things don't come up.

The trouble with growing old is that the safe private places tend to shrink, as aging folks need more and more help with more and more private needs. To be in a hospital or to live in an assisted-living facility is to have other people knowing and overseeing basically everything about your body. The more we can respect an elderly person's basic privacy (even in the smallest ways), the better.

One important way in which we adult children can guard the dignity of our parents is to raise a generation after us that treats the generation before us with respect. This means we need regularly to connect our own children and grandchildren (or the younger generations in the church) with our parents (or with the older generations in the church), in order to teach them how to honor their elders. In my experience, teens especially are tempted to laugh at older people who can't follow the quick repartee of conversation, who have funny hairstyles, who move awkwardly, who get food on their faces, who misspeak the name of one of their grandchildren. We need to teach growing young people to grow in love and respect for their elders, to laugh with and not at them, to ask to hear their thoughts and stories, to listen well, and, in general, to treat them with dignity. How about the basics of teaching young people to stand when an older person arrives, or to offer a comfortable seat?

This isn't just a duty; it's also a joy. Children of all ages do take joy in relationships with elderly people when they make time for them. They quickly learn to love and respect their grandparents and their elders, as they interact with them and pray for them and share gifts with them and care for them in various ways. They learn from the stories old people love to tell. They see them die, and they grieve and think and learn about life and death.

This is ultimately the beauty of the church: we believers in Christ are meant to live in close contact with the generations around us, as God's love in Christ is passed on from one generation to the next. We are all pivots in the flow. In effect, we adult children are training the next generation to care well for us when we are old! What a humbling thought—but one that challenges us to honor our elders well, even in the most practical ways.

Consistently Respect Work

We've said that we can honor our elders by patiently respecting their personhood and carefully respecting their dignity. We can also honor them by *consistently respecting their good work.*

This is not a book about retirement, but, if it were, I would want to redefine that term as it is commonly used: as a cessation of work or a long vacation! Others have spoken wisely on this subject.[1] Part of the way we human beings reflect the God who made us in his image is through our work. God worked to create the world: "On the seventh day God finished his *work* that he had done, and he rested on the seventh day from all his *work* that he had done"

1. I recommend John Piper's little book *Rethinking Retirement: Finishing Life for the Glory of Christ* (Wheaton, IL: Crossway, 2009), as well as John Dunlop's *Retiring Well: Strategies for Finding Balance, Setting Priorities, and Glorifying God* (Wheaton, IL: Crossway, 2022).

(Gen. 2:2). And then God took the man he had made and "put him in the garden of Eden to *work* it and keep it" (Gen. 2:15). We human beings reflect our Maker in our work of all kinds.

What's more, as redeemed followers of Christ, we work for him, by his power and for his glory: "We are his workmanship, created in Christ Jesus for good works, which God prepared beforehand, that we should walk in them" (Eph. 2:10). Walking in those good works by the power of Christ does not end in this life, for as long as we are consciously able.

To honor another human being at any stage of life, then, is to honor and respect his or her work—and to encourage that work to continue as richly as God allows, to the end. Undoubtedly, the work people do at eighty or ninety years old may be different from the work they did earlier in their lives. Often, however, the abilities that enabled them to work when they were younger can flow forward into different channels.

In my mother's retirement community lives an elderly resident who worked for years in various fields of developing technology; he now spends his days visiting and caring for his wife, who suffers from dementia—you see him regularly wheeling her around. But he also makes it his business to help other residents with their technological needs, which are many! Over a decade ago, when my father was struggling to make sense of word processing, this man came and helped him understand his computer. Just recently, when my mother had to spend a few months in the skilled care unit, this man accompanied me to her assisted-living apartment, helped me disconnect and transport her TV and the headset she needs to hear it, and reconnected them in her skilled care room. And now he's helped her put it all back together in her assisted-living quarters. I am eternally grateful for his good work.

My mother used to direct church choirs; in her earlier years in the retirement community, she directed and later sang in the resident choir, which performs amazing music. Some of the residents tutor children from the local schools. Many regularly write notes to others. My mother used to do a good bit of writing; now, every month, she dictates to me the messages she would like to write in various cards, I do the writing, and we get them mailed off, with a sense of satisfaction. It may seem little, but it is good work.

Most of all, now, Mom prays for people, especially for her family members. She does the good work of prayer. She gets in bed every night and tries to say the names of all nineteen of her great-grandchildren and pray for them one by one. That is good work, for as long as she is able to do it. She is still bearing fruit in old age, even as the psalmist explains:

> The righteous flourish like the palm tree
> and grow like a cedar in Lebanon.
> They are planted in the house of the Lord;
> they flourish in the courts of our God.
> They still bear fruit in old age;
> they are ever full of sap and green,
> to declare that the Lord is upright;
> he is my rock, and there is no unrighteousness in him.
> (Ps. 92:12–15)

How shall we honor our parents and elders as they journey through the years of their old age? Trusting in our heavenly Father and aiming ultimately to honor him, we honor our parents and elders by patiently respecting their personhood, carefully respecting their dignity, and consistently respecting their work.

By Grace Alone

In this discussion of honoring parents, there will be those who raise their hand (or who wish they could do so) and say, "But what about the parent who mistreated or abused me? Is that parent worthy of honor?" Oh, what a hard question this is, one that is always asked in the context of painful experience. In cases of abuse, children (and grandchildren) must often be physically distant from parents (or grandparents) who cannot be trusted as safe. Abuse by a parent is evil, and we must never even begin to rationalize or justify such wickedness as we deal with it.

But I wonder if the basic principles put forth here still apply: must we not respect the personhood of a parent lost in sin, praying for the soul of that person who gave us life and who needs above all to know the Lord who can give him or her life? How can we extend to that parent as much dignity as possible, speaking and living hard truth while pointing the way to faith in a God who forgives us through his Son? Answers to such questions are not easy. Lord, show us the way. Only by the Lord's supernatural strength can we trust that he alone will accomplish perfect justice in the end. Only through the power of the Holy Spirit can we show our heavenly Father's love to a parent who has abused rather than loved us.

Lived-out honor to a parent or elder is a potent witness to the world around us, more than we might imagine. It often happens in little ways. Almost every time I take my mother for outings in her wheelchair, whether for a meal or a trip to the mall, we are approached by someone who asks us, usually in a wondering kind of way, whether we are mother and daughter. They'll often say something like, "It is just beautiful to see you having such a good time together." It happened not long ago, when we had been laughing loud as we clumsily attempted to try on some clothes in the small dressing room crowded by the wheelchair. It often happens when we visit her favorite buffet with all the home-cooked Amish food, and I know just what special foods to bring her for the various courses.

To me and to my mother, this all feels like normal, messy life. But to others, it's clear that this kind of happy interaction at this stage somehow stands out. When a person speaks to us, my mother usually straightens up, lights up, and starts enthusiastically detailing our family history, my husband's and my travel schedules, and the titles of the books I've written—all of which irritates me greatly.

But it's all good. It's good to see her light up. This is a parent I aim to honor, and the Lord knows I don't always succeed. May his grace keep working on the bent of my heart. May the Lord help us honor our parents.

5

God Sees the Sufferings of Age

In the final chapter of the Old Testament wisdom book of Ecclesiastes, the writer in poetic lines makes vivid and heartbreaking the sufferings and sorrows of old age. It is a remarkable moment in God's breathed-out Word, as the Lord takes time to show us how deeply he understands the struggles of growing old. The first two big biblical truths we encountered pointed us to a sovereign Lord who rules over the aging process and who commands us how to live in light of it, honoring our elders. The third big biblical truth now draws us closer in, to witness God's eyes for the sufferings of age. It is important that God sees these sufferings—and that we see them through his eyes.

Out of Sight, but Not Forgotten

The sufferings of old age are often out of sight and forgotten. It is, for me, one of the saddest parts of this stage of life that my mother is not seen more often by other family members. I have grappled with the question of whether we should have insisted after my father's death that she move from one part of the country to another in order to be closer to us and to the whole clan. She did not want to leave all her familiar places and friends, and we understood. It might not have worked; we reasoned that, with her impaired vision and her hesitancy, she might not have been able to handle the transition. These are the kinds of questions with which we children struggle, and there is no simple answer. The ultimate answer is to rest all our decisions in the sovereignty and the goodness of our Lord who sees our paths from beginning to end.

We can learn from our decisions, however. These days, I often urge my friends to weigh carefully the factor of geographical proximity in their decisions regarding how to guide their parents and how much to insist that they be close to family. It seems like an obvious factor, but it is one that must be considered as early on as possible in the aging process: with every passing year, it becomes harder and harder for elderly folks to change place. And, for an older person, a change of fifteen miles can be as unsettling as a change of a thousand miles. Certainly we cannot predict where various family members will live, but we can do our best to help our parents settle close to their loved ones. For the elderly in the church, especially those without children, proximity to loved ones in the church family is equally important. Aging folks need to be seen in the flesh.

This kind of proximity lends caregivers many practical advantages: regular check-ins and oversight of care, immediate physical response to emergencies, ease for family members and friends in stopping by or taking an elderly loved one for an outing. But such benefits aren't merely practical—together, they foster an overall closeness of life that simply cannot be re-created from afar. Even with phone calls to Mom morning and night, even with visits every few weeks, even with empathizing as fully as possible with her updates regarding experiences, pains, joys, and concerns . . . it's not the same as the regular sharing of community, relationships, ordinary meals, children's chatter, everyday pains, moments of spontaneous laughter. Hearing about Mom's arthritic hip is much different from actually helping her up out of a chair and seeing her struggle.

Recently, one of our sons, his wife, and their four children accompanied my husband and me on a trip to visit Grandma / Great Grandma. They had not been able to see her for a long while. It was amazing to witness their interaction; each child was so kind to this elderly great-grandmother they had prayed for and sent notes to and called on the phone. They took turns pushing her wheelchair. They loved chatting with her—and they spoke up nice and loud when she couldn't hear. They listened attentively to her stories of generations past. They hugged her, and they cried when they left because they could see she was sad to be left alone.

The point is simply that old age, with all its various sufferings, needs live witnesses. Too many elderly folks are shut away in living situations that lack the ordinary kinds of interaction through which they are seen, known, and remembered. The truth is, however, that no matter how hard we try, we imperfect human beings can never be adequate witnesses. We will never see and know and remember well enough. With these acknowledgements, we are prepared to turn to Ecclesiastes 12, a passage in which we read that God sees; God knows; God remembers. The record is right here in his Word.

God Sees Old Age

The poetic lines in Ecclesiastes 12:1–8 are not addressed to aging people; they're part of a call to *young* people to remember God while there is still time. "Remember also your Creator in the days of your youth," says the Preacher, "before the evil days come" (Eccl. 12:1). The "evil days" are then described: they are the days of old age when the body breaks down and dies. The passage calls us to look early and urgently to the God who made us, for our chance to do so will not last long.

The whole book of Ecclesiastes highlights the transience of earthly life: we humans come and go like a seemingly meaningless vapor, a vain breath that gains nothing in the end (see Eccl. 1:1–11).

From its opening words, this book captures and expresses this sense of futility, the meaninglessness, or "vanity," that human beings feel when we try on our own to make sense of life and death and generations and seasons . . . all these endless cycles that seem to lead nowhere.

Ecclesiastes does not leave us alone with this sense of futility; it acknowledges and finally focuses on the God who created and oversees all things, the one to whom we must look in reverence and fear. But along with the truth about God comes the true experience of grappling with this fallen world, where everything passes away. Death is everywhere. If there is a book that truly shows the judgment of death given to Adam and Eve, and so to all the human race, Ecclesiastes is that book.

In the process of calling people to remember their Creator while they are young, the Preacher of Ecclesiastes paints a memorable and painful portrait of old age. How intriguing, that God wants young people really to *see* the reality of old age, with all its physical sufferings. They need to see it; we all need to see it better than we do. If we are not yet old, reading Ecclesiastes 12 shines light on the arc of our earthly lives that will end in meeting our Creator. If we are old, reading these words will strangely comfort us: God knows and names this particular suffering of an aged body breaking down. God sees us in the midst of it and sustains us to the end.

It is good to reread this section of Scripture before thinking about it, for it is almost shocking in its beautiful portrayal of such a painful reality:

> Remember also your Creator in the days of your youth, before the evil days come and the years draw near of which you will say, "I have no pleasure in them"; before the sun and the light and the moon and the stars are darkened and the clouds return after the rain, in the day when the keepers of the house tremble, and the strong men are bent, and the grinders cease because they are few, and those who look through the windows are

> dimmed, and the doors on the street are shut—when the sound of the grinding is low, and one rises up at the sound of a bird, and all the daughters of song are brought low—they are afraid also of what is high, and terrors are in the way; the almond tree blossoms, the grasshopper drags itself along, and desire fails, because man is going to his eternal home, and the mourners go about the streets—before the silver cord is snapped, or the golden bowl is broken, or the pitcher is shattered at the fountain, or the wheel broken at the cistern, and the dust returns to the earth as it was, and the spirit returns to God who gave it. Vanity of vanities, says the Preacher; all is vanity. (Eccl. 12:1–8)

The phrases come not in the traditional parallelism of Hebrew poetry but rather in a long stream of imagery—almost like one cry after another, in one extended lament. The only words actually given to the aging person are the first ones, concerning these later years: "I have no pleasure in them." How finally sad: pleasure in life is gone.

The pictures that follow tell us why, as the portrait of a decaying household communicates the physical decay of old age. In this scene, the sun and light and moon and stars are all dark; even after the rain come only more clouds. The "keepers of the house" probably picture trembling arms and hands that can no longer hold anything securely. The "strong men" portray old legs that are bent, no longer able to carry the weight of a body. The "grinders" cease, being few: aged people who have lost a lot of teeth cannot chew or enjoy their food. Indeed, older people often just lose their appetite and, sadly, take no joy in the simple, regular pleasure of eating. Old eyes are windows through which one sees only dimly. This person feels closed off from the outer world—as if the doors to the house have been shut (which may suggest ears that do not let in sound).

The remaining images help communicate not just the decay itself but the sense of alienation and fear an elderly person often feels, behind those shut doors. Verse 4 is all about sound and hearing: first, "the sound of the grinding is low," and, finally, "all the daughters of song are brought low": an elderly person who has lost a good bit of hearing strains to hear all kinds of common everyday sounds, as well as beautiful sounds.

We might recall old Barzillai the Gileadite, who rejected David's offer of a pleasurable stay in Jerusalem, asking whether David thought that he, at his advanced age, would actually be able to taste all the good food or enjoy the voices of the singers (see 2 Sam. 19:35). Think of how a person with normal hearing simply enjoys listening to music—and then imagine the experience of straining and straining to catch the melody or the words, as if the volume button on a TV just doesn't work. I've witnessed in many elderly loved ones the ways hearing loss can bring frustration, embarrassment, and distance, all of which multiply as the loss increases.

In the middle of Ecclesiastes 12:4 comes a startling small sound that *is* heard: an elderly person does not sleep well and so "rises up at the sound of a bird." His rest is that tenuous and breakable, even though his hearing is that poor. For an elderly person sleep is a relief, but it is so often and so easily interrupted—by noise, by the body's needs, and on and on. This section makes me think of the ordinary but sometimes truly terrifying experience of an aged person waking up in the night (or maybe in the early hours just before dawn) and creeping gingerly into the next room, probably the bathroom. I picture my mother moving slowly through the dark, afraid to fall down again, or to have something fall on her—fearing "terrors . . . in the way."

The passage completes the portrait with pictures of the white hair of old age ("the almond tree blossoms"); slow shuffling feet, perhaps with a cane ("the grasshopper drags itself along"); and the complete loss of sexual interest or capacity ("desire fails"). A blossoming almond tree usually suggests fruit to come, and a grasshopper usually hops up rather than dragging itself on the ground: these surprising and memorable images almost ironically highlight the ravages of old age, when the body will no longer do what we always expected it to do.

As the poet draws his imagery from the natural world around him, he well expresses the universal human experience of the body's eventual decline. Through these poignant pictures, we understand that we are witnessing not a little thing but something that echoes loudly and sorrowfully throughout creation. We recall Isaiah's message of God's sovereignty: God "sits above the circle of the earth, and its inhabitants are like grasshoppers" (Isa. 40:22). The Preacher of Ecclesiastes would remind us that this sovereign God sees and cares about every detail and every stage of each grasshopper's life.

Returning to Dust

The word "because" (Eccl. 12:5) connects us to the final reality of old age: old age leads to death. Even for those fortunate ones who do not experience a debilitating decline as they age, the eventual end of death is sure.

Death is pictured here with a remarkable assortment of images that are flanked with eternal truths on either side: "man is going to his eternal home" (v. 5), and "the dust returns to the earth as it was, and the spirit returns to God who gave it" (v. 7). Well should mourners fill the streets (see v. 5), as the picture widens to show the magnitude of this sorrow. The dust signals that this is creation undone: the writer's description here harks back to the very beginning, when God formed Adam "of dust from the ground and breathed into his nostrils the breath of life" (Gen. 2:7). It is because God made us from dust that Psalm 103:13–14 is true:

> As a father shows compassion to his children,
> so the Lord shows compassion to those who fear him.
> For he knows our frame;
> he remembers that we are dust.

Within the bookends of these eternal truths, two pairs of images depict the transition from physical life to death. The images are again almost ironically full of beauty and life—but beauty and life broken and cut off. Ecclesiastes 12:6 describes things of great value, shining things that sustain and hold what is precious. But the silver cord snaps, and the golden bowl is broken. The pitcher at the fountain is shattered, and the wheel that moves the water is ruined; this second pair of images shows people being cut off from the water that gives them life. Words like *snaps* and *broken* and *shattered* make us feel the grievous, jolting transition from life to death.

In response to this climactic portrait of brokenness, the Preacher finally repeats his theme: "Vanity of vanities . . . all is vanity" (12:8). Hasn't this depiction of old age and death given the final evidence? Human life in this fallen world is truly like a breath, a vapor that appears and passes away. Ecclesiastes presents a most masterful lament for its passing.

We might be relieved when we finally come to the end of this lament, which asks us to suffer an almost exhausting series of pictures that powerfully invade our imaginations with the reality of physical decline. Arms . . . legs . . . teeth . . . eyes . . . ears . . . *everything* fails. What a depressing passage, we might say. It makes the same assault on our senses that we experience after spending long hours in the skilled care unit of a retirement community, seeing all those bodies so frail and failing. Walking down a long hall and glancing past the half-shut doors, it's just one poor body after another after another.

How should we respond? As I've studied Ecclesiastes with various Bible study groups, the responses to this passage have been varied. One woman, on first reading, just couldn't believe that these pictures are actually intended by God to show the physical decline of old age. Indeed, on first reading, they might take us aback, or even shock us. We might not think God would have spoken this way about the elderly, exposing their physical decline so extensively. Today's more popular version of compassion would try to cover it up or put it away.

After the initial shock, however, most readers respond with sorrow for the fallen human condition, wonder at the way these words capture this stage of it, and often even comfort in the fact that God sees and says it. They hear God giving shape and expression either to their own physical struggles or to those of elderly loved ones. To put such struggles into words, such beautiful words, gives them lasting meaning.

God's compassion overflows as he truly sees and names our suffering. It would not be compassionate to pretend the suffering is not there, or to portray it as less than it is. It is not compassionate to avoid spending time in that skilled care unit, much as it assaults our senses. In his infinite compassion, God leads us to confront the reality of death and eternity, so that we turn to him, our only hope. We have much to learn from the magnitude of God's compassion; it is greater than we made-from-dust human beings can comprehend.

In compassion, God sees and says the full truth of an aging person's suffering; no one else can. The aging one often cannot grasp it fully or communicate it clearly. He may hear the words of Ecclesiastes 12 and know they are true, but inside the breaking-down house with the dimmed windows and the closed doors, the big picture is not accessible. Aging happens to us gradually, and aging ones can be so preoccupied with adjusting to each new stage of struggle or loss that they cannot hold the whole process in their minds; perhaps that is one small comfort. But that is also one crucial reason young people must see and hear these truths, while their eyes and ears are wide open.

God Sees Us through Suffering and Death

This portrayal of physical decline and death is not the end of the book or the end of the story, as we believers well know. It is important, however, to stop and read and see what these verses on old age show us. They give us a witness, God's own witness, to the true experience of aging—specifically to the body's decay.

In the aging process the physical reality claims our attention, and rightly so. The body dies, not the spirit. In the decline and death of the body, we humans more deeply understand God's creation of us as spiritual but *embodied* beings—ordained to live in the unity of flesh and spirit for eternity. The rending of that unity in physical death should call forth mourners indeed. Our bodies are an eternal part of who we are. We love these human bodies that God made, and God loves them, too. We suffer a most terrible snapping, breaking, tearing of physical from spiritual in the decay and death of our bodies. Our God sees and understands this deep, awful divide.

But God's creation purposes will not be thwarted. Here we must state again our Christian hope, which will be explored in more detail in a later chapter. But this hope must be clear at every point; the hope lights up the suffering in a multitude of ways. We believers do not grieve "as others do who have no hope" (1 Thess. 4:13). Our hope applies the only effective salve to the suffering and death of human bodies.

The Scriptures assure us that, when Christ returns to earth, the bodies of all believers will be resurrected from the grave just as Christ's own body was resurrected: he is the "firstfruits" of many (1 Cor. 15:20). The Westminster Larger Catechism affirms that at death the souls of believers are "made perfect in holiness, and received into the highest heavens," in the very presence of Christ our Savior; it affirms an equally glorious truth about their bodies, which "even in death continue united to Christ, and rest in their graves as in their beds, till at the last day they be again united to their souls."[1] We will be perfectly made whole. Resurrected, eternal life with Jesus Christ our Lord is the certain hope of those who have been made new through faith in his saving work on our behalf.

1. Westminster Larger Catechism, answer 86.

Such a hope is the ultimate reason human beings can survive and even triumph over physical suffering and death. We know that the snapping of the cord is not permanent; it will be mended and more beautiful than ever, forever. We can trust God to do this. "Consider the work of God: who can make straight what he has made crooked?" (Eccl. 7:13). By implication, only the God who made it all and judged it all can put it all back together perfectly; God alone will finally complete the straightening he has accomplished through his Son on the cross.

Until then, his children by faith have been made new: the pitcher is shattered, but we have in Jesus a never-ending "spring of water welling up to eternal life" (John 4:14). Nothing, not even death, can separate us from the love of Christ (see Rom. 8:38–39). We belong to him now and forever. This is why we can read Ecclesiastes 12 in faith and not despair. This is why the apostle Paul can speak of not losing heart in the midst of bodily sufferings:

> Though our outer self is wasting away, our inner self is being renewed day by day. For this light momentary affliction is preparing for us an eternal weight of glory beyond all comparison, as we look not to the things that are seen but to the things that are unseen. For the things that are seen are transient, but the things that are unseen are eternal. (2 Cor. 4:16–18)

In the meantime, though, we human beings suffer the awful snapping, breaking, tearing of physical from spiritual in the decay and death of our transient bodies during those "evil days" Ecclesiastes describes. Through this suffering we sense the depths of sin and the fall; we learn to measure evil by God's judgment of it. Through this suffering we also sense the depths of God's grace, that he should give his Son to suffer in our place the tearing apart of both physical death and spiritual death—so that we need not know the separation from God that is hell.

God ordains and intimately knows our suffering now and to the end of this earthly life, but God's redemptive purpose is to deliver his people from eternal suffering by giving them eternal life when they place their faith in Christ our Lord. God's compassion is eternal compassion. God sees our human suffering and tells us so through a Word that tells our whole story, to the very end.

I had a childhood friend who lived just a few houses away. Our families attended the same church, so we spent many hours together. When we were just young teens, my friend's mother developed cancer and was confined to her bed for several months before she died. Her bedroom was down the hall from their living room, where they had a piano, and when I visited during her months of confinement, she would often ask us to sing hymns for her—I would play, and we both would sing through the verses of many a hymn for this dear sick mom hidden away down the hall. I cannot see her face in my mind today, but I can still hear one hymn she often requested. Written by the great hymnist Fanny Crosby, it begins like this:

> Some day the silver cord will break,
> And I no more as now shall sing;
> But, O the joy when I shall wake
> Within the palace of the King!

Then comes the chorus:

> And I shall see Him face to face,
> And tell the story, saved by grace:
> And I shall see Him face to face,
> And tell the story, saved by grace.[2]

2. Fanny Crosby, "Saved by Grace," 1891.

As we young girls sang this hymn, I had only the vaguest idea of what it might mean for the silver cord to break. The image was striking, but the reality was distant. Indeed, death is seldom a vital reality for youth. They have to grow and learn. What a blessing, to grow and learn.

The Preacher of Ecclesiastes says, *Learn early*! Remember your Creator in the days of your *youth*! Wisdom comes from God, who sees and oversees the entire human story: he created all things in the beginning, and he will judge all things in the end. With this truth the book concludes:

> Fear God and keep his commandments, for this is the whole duty of man. For God will bring every deed into judgment, with every secret thing, whether good or evil. (Eccl. 12:13–14)

This is the God who sees, now and forever.

Nothing in the universe happens apart from the all-seeing eye of God. This includes what happens in a dark little bedroom where a bent-over, white-haired person made in God's image wakes up, laboriously climbs out from under the covers, grabs on to a walker for help, and creeps like a grasshopper toward the bathroom. God sees and cares about this human being he made; he takes time to talk about it in his revealed Word, in the most beautiful possible language. In the next chapter, we will consider how we might grow to see and care more and more, like God does, for those suffering the physical decline of old age.

6

Responding with Compassion

The third big biblical truth we've been focusing on is this: God sees the sufferings of old age. To grasp this truth we've listened to Ecclesiastes 12, in which the inspired writer vividly communicates the stark reality of such suffering—so that young people might see it and fear God early, and so that we all might understand how deeply God sees us. The question for this chapter is how we who care for aging loved ones can develop eyes like God's for their sufferings and respond with compassion like God's to the struggles of old age.

Let's consider three ways in which younger people often refuse to see and respond compassionately; we'll answer each negative with a positive, to grasp how we can aim to follow our Creator in seeing and caring for aging loved ones. But we start with negatives, mainly because examples are so easy to find and tempting to follow.

One of the reasons the book of Ecclesiastes speaks so powerfully is that it cuts with truth into the blind, busy routines of life that tend to take over our day-to-day existence; in general, we are not good at stopping to see through to ultimate reality and to respond appropriately. That's one thing old age and dying does: it halts us and asks us to confront life and death in a fundamental, often jolting way.

To Pretend, or to Be True

The first way many of us avoid true seeing and compassionate responding is to pretend—to pretend in various ways that the reality of old age is not really what it is. We talked earlier about the ways in which we today are tempted and even encouraged to deny the reality of old age and death; the subject bears further discussion, particularly in light of the need to show compassion that is true, like God's, not false, like that of many in the world around us.

One of the most powerful literary portrayals of such pretense comes from Leo Tolstoy, in his novella *The Death of Iván Ilých*: the story of a conventional, status-seeking court justice in nineteenth-century Russia who is suddenly forced to confront his own disease and death.[1]

The story opens with a glimpse of Iván's friends and coworkers from the courts of St. Petersburg, who learn of Iván's death and must then attend the wake at his home. From their point of view, we feel the bothersome interruption of their pleasant schedules, their discomfort in front of the laid-out corpse in an upstairs room, their awkward exchanges with Iván's widow—and their quick-as-possible exit in order to make it in time to their evening game of bridge. The story starts with the pretenders. Only a little pink stool called a *pouffe*, the springs of which squeak obtrusively when one of Iván's friends sits or moves on it, seems to poke fun at the pretentious people filling the well-decorated house.

The narrative then shifts, however, to the story of Iván's life from his own perspective, tracing his quite predictable journey along the road of professional and societal success until, at a point in midlife when he should be enjoying that success, he suffers a minor fall from a ladder while supervising the decoration of their

1. Leo Tolstoy, *The Death of Iván Ilých*, in *Eleven Modern Short Novels*, 2nd ed., Leo Hamalian and Edmond L. Volpe (New York: Putnam, 1970), 3–61.

new house. Life from all appearances moves on pleasantly, but his internal injury from that fall develops into an incurable, increasingly painful condition that eventually takes his life—although not before agonizingly opening his eyes to the meaninglessness of the success that consumed his life. In the end, Iván mercifully ceases to pretend; deep inside himself he faces the truth of who he is and how greatly he has missed the mark of that truth. Perhaps that is why his face from the coffin at the wake seems to offer "a reproach and a warning to the living."[2]

As his disease progresses, Iván suffers deeply from the pretense of those around him: friends, doctors, and especially his family. Friends avoid the subject of his illness, doctors use vague terminology and keep ordering more and different pills and treatments, and family try to soothe him while fitting him into their schedules—which are filled with nice dinners, visits to the opera, and an eligible suitor courting his daughter. The eventual ugliness of his sickness, with its messes and smells, does not fit with the decorum of their lives, as he well knows; he lived that decorum. They pat his covers, stress that he must take his pills to get better, and lament the fact that such a terrible thing could happen to them. They do not speak of death. They do not imagine the inner journey Iván is making.

If you haven't, you should read the story; it is powerful. Tolstoy has given us a fictional but vividly true account of a dying person's journey toward reality. I stress here not just the journey but also the role of those who should help the journeyer on his way, his wife and children in particular.

We'll come back to that story in a moment. For now, let's stop and consider our tendency toward pretense in the face of one whose body is in decline. Maybe we'd rather not talk of such things. Maybe we think it's encouraging to insist that the medicine will work.

2. Tolstoy, 6.

Sometimes it will. But in the case of a ninety-something-year-old mother, for example, it often will not.

When my mother brings up her various sufferings—arthritis, or her worsening vision—my immediate tendency is to try to say something encouraging, something that will make her pain seem not so bad. I'm a glass-half-full person by nature. "Well, at least we can be thankful, Mom, that you can see as much as you can." "Well, Mom, I am so glad you have the best doctor, one who will know right away if they discover something that will help."

Sometimes these sorts of comments are accepted well, or at least without dispute. But, increasingly, I'm learning that it's probably just as comforting to listen well and to give assent to my mother's experience—simply acknowledging that her suffering is real. The glass *is* also half empty. "Yes, I'm so sorry that your good eye is a bit weaker lately. That must be so hard." Actually, offering a comment like that first can help pave the way for an encouraging comment to follow.

To try to avoid true suffering, or to pretend that the suffering is less than it is, does not help; it only leaves the sufferer to suffer alone. How much better to name the suffering. It is better indeed (although more labor-intensive) to stop and imagine the suffering person's journey, to share it for a moment, and then to help deal with the suffering as best we can. In so doing, we more truly show compassion, and we also stretch our minds and hearts to think and care more like God does.

As to death itself, how much better to name it and help our loved one face it, rather than to avoid its reality and its magnitude. Death will break in and mock all our pretenses. The springs of that pink pouffe in Tolstoy's story just keep squeaking, in the most unseemly way, there in that carefully decorated room full of well-dressed people —and with a well-dressed corpse in the adjoining room. The silver cord will snap, and the golden bowl will break. If our loved one is an unbeliever, there is no compassion in enabling him or her to avoid thinking about the reality of dying and facing our Creator God.

John Piper has famously encouraged Christians to care about all suffering, *especially* eternal suffering.[3]

How we confront and name the reality of death is so, so sensitive, to be sure. One of my friends asked her unbelieving mother if she could simply read psalms aloud to her for a bit each day; her mother happened to love poetry. And so they came to talk about the valley of the shadow of death. Hearing the Word, any part of the living and active Word, is key.

The Scriptures put forward the subject of death throughout their pages, from the punishment of sin by death in the first chapters, to the required bloody sacrifices in the temple, to the climax of Jesus's death on our behalf and resurrection from the dead, to the culminating scene in Revelation where Death is thrown into the lake of fire forever. John's warning in that final book of the Bible is so clear: "If anyone's name was not found written in the book of life, he was thrown into the lake of fire" (Rev. 20:15).

How do we approach such subjects? Prayer opens the way. Communing with God as we read his Word is the most powerful help in communing with aged loved ones. God answers our prayers. He will show us the times to be quiet and the times to speak with them about this gospel that gives us eternal life instead of eternal death through Jesus our Savior.

We believers cannot arrange the perfect time or way to speak, but we can pray, both alone and alongside the believers around us, for the Spirit to move like the invisible wind in the conversations we are given with folks who are approaching the end of their lives on this earth. Such conversations are sacred space, to be treasured and covered in prayer. When we do not even know how to pray, we have divine and perfect help. Here is the greatest comfort:

3. John Piper, "Abortion and the Narrow Way That Leads to Life," Desiring God, January 23, 2011, https://www.desiringgod.org/messages/abortion-and-the-narrow-way-that-leads-to-life.

> The Spirit helps us in our weakness. For we do not know what to pray for as we ought, but the Spirit himself intercedes for us with groanings too deep for words. And he who searches hearts knows what is the mind of the Spirit, because the Spirit intercedes for the saints according to the will of God. (Rom. 8:26–27)

Of course, we must *always* be praying for opportunities to tell the good news of the gospel, as we do not know which people around us will die sooner than later. Death shocks and surprises us all the time—indeed, it is amazing that we continue to be shocked and surprised. But in our blindness and oblivion, we can pray for opportunities to play a part in God's big plan to thwart death, finally and ultimately, through the death and resurrection of his own Son on our behalf.

Among aging folks this need is blatantly urgent, and the opportunities are many. We can take this urgency to God, who hears our prayers and helps us to speak truth in situations we could never imagine or manipulate by ourselves. We can bring our loved ones to church, or under the ministry of a church, or into the presence of believers who know and speak biblical truth about God. We can read or speak the Word to them.

Speaking truth is always better than pretending. Speaking truth is true compassion. Speaking truth is ultimately a matter of life and death—eternal life and death.

To Coddle, or to Be Straightforward

The call to respond with true compassion can easily be misunderstood or misused by those who struggle to speak truth calmly and confidently. Even when we don't pretend concerning the reality of suffering and death, we can sometimes exude a kind of sympathy that misses the mark, smothering rather than strengthening.

Years ago, during my first experience of labor before giving birth, my husband and I were visited by one tearful acquaintance just as complications arose and we had to make decisions about how to proceed. The last thing I needed right then was a weeping companion who pitied me as a victim going to the slaughter. Her visit was kindly meant, but I was relieved when she left and left me to the straightforward help of my husband, a truth-speaker without frills—which is often the very best comfort.

The second way, then, in which we can refuse to see and respond with true compassion is to display a kind of sympathy that does not directly address the suffering and the particular needs right in front of our eyes; it is a show of emotion or action that is sometimes more self-centered than other-centered. The solicitous bustle of Iván's family, as they pat his covers and urge him to take his pills, is in truth a way to dispose of him conveniently so that they can get on with their schedules. They are indeed lamenting the fact that such a terrible thing could have happened to *them*.

Probably all of us have offered this kind of sympathy at one time or another. I've called it *coddling*, for lack of a better word; it often relies on style and outward show rather than on truly seeing and addressing a person's needs. It puts on a display of general sadness, but not one applicable to a particular person's particular situation. This kind of sympathy does not truly comfort.

It is not simple to find the best way to show compassion to one who is suffering. I understand from stories of friends that my husband and I are not unusual in that we often disagree regarding how best to express true compassion to my mother. I tend to let my mother worry or fuss over something she is upset about, waiting her out and then trying to reason with her. My husband would speak into her worries sooner rather than later, stating the truth of the situation and calling her to acknowledge the facts and depend on the Lord to deal with them. If she needs to be pushed in the wheelchair to a church service rather than laboriously (and dangerously) making her way with her walker, as she would rather be able to do, then there is not much benefit in painfully drawing out a discussion of the matter; that simply escalates the tension—which is not truly compassionate.

In general, my husband's plain way is usually better, although a few "frills," gentle frills, never hurt. Of course, we carefully choose how much to share with Mom, and when, according to her ability to process all the details. It's an ongoing learning process for us, one in which we need to help each other, as we learn to give true help to our aging loved ones.

These issues are important for caregivers to discuss, especially among family members involved in the care of an elderly loved one. I am my mother's only surviving child, without siblings with whom to share my mother's care—but also without the tensions that often arise among siblings in these matters. My husband and I regularly talk over the details of Mom's care, our handling of her finances, the schedule for our visits, and so forth—and it is complicated enough. It is a matter of agreeing (or agreeing to disagree) concerning just how to view Mom's needs and respond with godly compassion, as the Lord gives us wisdom together.

I often hear from friends who clash with siblings and/or spouses concerning appropriate responses to the needs of an aging parent. One may feel that the others don't do enough, or don't do it right. Constant communication and prayer are urgently needed to care well and care together for loved ones in their old age.

The approach of calm, straightforward compassion helps caregivers work together to offer real support, as we speak truth to one another and to the elderly ones under our care. I've observed the nurses and aides in my mother's assisted-living unit: the ones who put on excessive shows of pity or other emotions quickly grow tiresome to everyone around them—especially to the elderly women and men who would rather hear a calm, understanding voice and receive a helping hand just when they need it.

My mother's favorite helper is the most matter-of-fact, down-to-earth woman, one who does not pretend Mom is weaker or stronger than she really is, who gives her the best rubdown and shampoo when she takes her for her bubble bath, and who quietly takes home and mends a blouse of Mom's that needs fixing. (She is better at that task than I am—and so she ministers to both of us.) Sometimes a helper like that comes along and gives us a lesson or two in compassionate care. It may not be a helper we would choose. But we do well to be grateful, and to listen and learn.

For elderly folks, little things are big things. If you tell my mother you're going to visit or call her at a certain time, every minute on the clock after that time is much longer than a minute. For many young people, a minute flies by and hardly counts; it is not so for our aged parents. To show compassion to them is to take great care for the seemingly little things that are big to them. (Just think how the world of us grasshoppers looks to our compassionate God.) Here is a great big little gift to an older person, a gift worth more than many flowery words: the gift of one person who faithfully shows up just when she says she will.

One person like that emerges in Tolstoy's story. Amid all the bustle and pretense that leaves Iván Ilých alone in his suffering, a household butler's assistant named Gerásim stands out. A strong young peasant lad from the countryside, Gerásim is devoid of pretense; he is the agent of truth in the narrative. He does not hesitate to clean up Iván's messes, and Iván comes to find comfort in the life and strength and kindness that naturally exude from this unpretentious fellow. When Gerásim holds up Iván's legs in a certain position, Iván feels better. Tolstoy's description says it all:

> Gerásim alone did not lie; everything showed that he alone understood the facts of the case and did not consider it necessary to disguise them, but simply felt sorry for his emaciated and enfeebled master. Once when Iván Ilých was sending him

> away he even said straight out: "We shall all of us die, so why should I grudge a little trouble?"—expressing the fact that he did not think his work burdensome, because he was doing it for a dying man and hoped someone would do the same for him when his time came.[4]

Iván Ilých is truly comforted by the honest compassion of this simple servant. Gerásim sees and says it straightforwardly; he is more like God than the pretenders around him. Indeed, we shall all of us die.

As we care for the aging, this is a valuable reminder. After a lifetime of experiences, elderly folks can smell a lack of straightforward concern and care, what younger generations would call "inauthenticity." They know when we're not really seeing them or addressing their needs. "Coddling" does not comfort. As we recall, the words of Ecclesiastes 12 do the opposite of coddling: in that passage, the speaker peers deeply into the painful experience of an aging body, and he expresses it truly (and helps gladly). In such expression (and such help) can be found great comfort.

To Patronize, or to Stand Alongside

The third way we can refuse to see and compassionately care for the sufferings of the elderly is to patronize them—that is, to put ourselves above them in some way. We might treat them like children, or resent them, or laugh at them. To define this attitude makes it sound so mean or unattractive that we might assume it could not apply to us; of course I would never act patronizingly superior to my mother, or laugh at her. And yet I do, sometimes.

Just the other day, as Mom on the phone was wishing for maybe the fiftieth time that my current trip out of the country would be

4. Tolstoy, *The Death of Iván Ilých*, 39.

shorter or would be over, I found myself responding in the tone one sometimes uses with an unruly child, speaking extra slowly and clearly and with a saccharine sweetness. It was a patronizing and not a compassionate tone, evidencing prideful heart attitudes for which I needed to repent. Indeed, any wrongful approach to compassion begins in our sinful, selfish hearts, as we replace the desire to please God with the desire to please ourselves.

Such heart struggles can be just as much of an issue, and sometimes more so, for the spouses of children caring for their parents as for the children themselves. Much as we know that when we marry, we marry into a whole family and are called to love our spouse's loved ones as our own, it is sometimes harder to care unselfishly for one who did not raise us. The relational bonds are not the same.

I should stop and qualify: sometimes this relational distance makes no difference—or even helps. I think I treated my mother-in-law with extra-special respect and care to the end, especially through her many years of widowhood, because, in a sense, I was always a guest in her home in a way that I am not a guest in my mother's home. I dig right in and organize my mom's closets more aggressively, and probably more insensitively, than I would have done for my mother-in-law. When we visited my mother-in-law, I would stay up and talk with her, no matter how tired I was, because she always wanted to hear right away about the children and grandchildren, whereas my husband (her son) felt free to go on to bed. (Of course, he would be awake way before dawn, and they would have their early-morning mother–son time chatting away over coffee.) Whatever our relational distance, we must aim to love our in-laws well!

A Hollywood movie titled *Make Way for Tomorrow* offers a remarkable glimpse into a Depression-era version of such intergenerational family struggles. Not many true and sensitive dramatic portrayals of the plight of aging parents exist, but this is definitely one of them—and a powerful one. In this film from 1937 directed by Leo McCarey, Victor Moore and Beulah Bondi portray sweet but burdensome elderly parents who were happily married for fifty years, raised a family, but then lost their house to the bank. The two do not fit well into their busy adult children's families and schedules and social circles, and they are gradually pushed into the corners of their children's worlds.

The story is not sentimentalized but rather movingly and uncomfortably real. There is not a happy ending. But in the midst of it all, the older husband and wife somehow maintain hearts of unselfish love. Watching this story unfold will make you laugh and squirm and probably weep. As good stories do, this one will make you see your own struggles a bit more clearly.

A couple we know well took the wife's aging parents into their home, and the husband shared quite candidly with us their struggles to "parent" especially his father-in-law, who was physically needy and not hesitant to talk about it. This son-in-law had to battle what he called his "critical eye" toward his father-in-law; in fact, both he and his wife struggled with the loss of space and privacy and all the daily sacrifices one has to make when caring for parents at home. But they did it together, willingly. He says he looks back on the years of that care as a "spiritual test that God used to teach and convict me of things in my life—but a blessing to be sure."

The blessing came as both this man and his wife humbled themselves before the Lord, realizing that, before God, they were both just as terribly needy as her parents. They spoke of how often they ran to the Lord to ask for forgiveness and hearts of love, and they asked brothers and sisters in Christ to pray with them. They cultivated hearts of thankfulness for all that their parents had given them throughout their lives, including a heritage of faith in Jesus Christ and a love for the church. They celebrated the sweet spirit of her mother, who, even with quickly developing dementia, continued to be joyful and trusting.

More and more, they came to understand, as they explained it, that if Jesus is preparing a mansion for sinners like them (see

John 14:2), then they should offer a little room in the house God entrusted to them on this earth. They considered how the time would probably come when they might need such help from their children. They embraced the ministry to which God called them, and God blessed them as they ministered faithfully—not perfectly, but faithfully—to their parents. God also blessed their friends and their children who witnessed their faithfulness.

A patronizing attitude is proud; the solution comes with humility before God. Humility calls us not to stand above our parents with critical, superior, or resentful spirits, but to stand alongside them, acknowledging that we are likewise needy, along with all God's creatures. We will laugh not at them but with them, for we are often foolish too. The pictures in Ecclesiastes will come true for us as well: the keepers of our house will tremble. As we stand alongside our parents, we can better look out on the world with them, helping them turn their eyes to needs larger than their own. We can help open those shut doors on the street, at least from time to time.

Here is one part of true compassion: expanding the vision of our parents, helping them keep sight of God's work in the world. We have acknowledged how an aged person's world can become smaller, so to speak—limited not just in place but also in focus, on one's body and one's pain and one's insistent daily needs. What a gift, to stand beside an aging person and share a glimpse of life outside of ourselves.

My mother and her friends love to hear about missionaries in other countries; they are some of the best "prayer warriors" in all the world. How good for the kingdom and the church—and how good as well for these aging folks who pray. Asking Mom to pray for another needy person, including me, is a great gift both for that person and for my mother. To make that ask helps keep us humble: it requires that we stand not above but alongside, sharing in our need before God in heaven, who made and rules us all. This is one rich benefit of regular prayer and worship, ideally within the fellowship of a church, where both we and our parents find ourselves alongside many brothers and sisters in the faith, celebrating God's perfect compassion for us sinners through Christ his Son.

God sees the whole span of each human life, through the sufferings of old age and to the very end. He is a compassionate God. Truly "he knows our frame; he remembers that we are dust" (Ps. 103:14). He knows our whole story, for he wrote it from the beginning. He sees us as we are, in our fallenness and need. And he sent his Son to save us. God's great compassion toward us changes the whole big story, and it must change each of the little stories that unfold within our own little households.

Echoing my friends who took in their parents, I preach these words to myself, especially in moments when I might be tempted to resent what can feel like a burdensome call on my time and energy: "If my heavenly Father gave his own Son to save a needy sinner like me, then how should I not reflect his compassion, even just a little bit, by giving my time and energy—and my true compassion—to care for the earthly father and mother he has given me?"

May we who are called to honor and care for our parents see them more and more with God's eyes and respond with compassion that is like his. May our compassion be not pretentious but true. May we not coddle but offer straightforward comfort. May we not patronize but rather come alongside our aging loved ones, fellow sinners in need of God's grace.

7

God Helps Us to the End

We have considered three big biblical truths so far: God's sovereign hand in the aging process, God's call to honor the aged, and God's eyes for the suffering of old age. The fourth truth we will consider is God's help to the end. It's a truth that has woven like a thread through the previous chapters; now let's pull it out and look at it.

If it weren't for this fourth truth, the first three might be too hard for us to accept. Yes, God sovereignly oversees old age and death as part of his judged, fallen creation—but he helps those who are experiencing the effects of that fallenness and promises to answer when they cry to him. Yes, God calls younger ones to honor the aged—but we cannot sufficiently lift them up ourselves; God is there as the ultimate help. Yes, God sees the sufferings of old age—but he does not simply see; he is there and ready to help the aged in their troubles.

A Present Help

To the end, it is true for believers that "God is our refuge and strength, a very present help in trouble" (Ps. 46:1). The emphasis on "very present" reminds us of God's eternal, unchanging nature:

we come and go, we weaken and die, but he is from everlasting to everlasting, always there in the present moment—the great "I AM" (Ex. 3:14). His help does not ebb and flow with people's ability to give or receive help. This is why the psalmist can say, "My flesh and my heart may fail, but God is the strength of my heart and my portion forever" (Ps. 73:26).

God's help to the end would seem to apply primarily to people who are aging. In caring for the elderly, however, I have come to see that this truth is as absolutely crucial for caregivers as for our aging loved ones. First and foremost, if our loved ones do not know the Lord God who has sent the ultimate and eternal help through his own Son, we caregivers are often the ones with the frontline opportunity to bring that good news to them and to pray for their salvation. If our loved ones do know the Lord through faith in Christ, then we get to point them to the help of their heavenly Father, praying with and for them as they seek that help.

It is also true, however, that we caregivers must ourselves learn to trust God's help for our loved ones. We can aim to be present and to honor and help them as much as possible—but only God can be the very present help that meets their deepest needs. God is the one who hears and answers that prayer of the psalmist: "Do not cast me off in the time of old age; forsake me not when my strength is spent" (Ps. 71:9).

I think of the Old Testament story of Jacob's wife Rachel, who so desperately wanted children. This was a family full of turmoil to begin with, as Jacob was also married to Rachel's sister Leah, who was having baby after baby after baby. Jacob loved Rachel more than he loved Leah, but he could not solve the problem of her barrenness. When Rachel went crying to him, "Give me children, or I shall die!" Jacob became angry and responded, "Am I in the place of God, who has withheld from you the fruit of the womb?" (Gen. 30:1, 2). It's a good question: *Am I in the place of God?* Jacob was telling Rachel that only the sovereign God could satisfy her desires; not Jacob but God himself was ultimately in charge of their story.

Spouses need to learn this truth. Parents need to learn this truth, for God is in charge of our children's stories. And grown children need to learn this truth, for God is in charge of our parents' stories. I can be as faithful as possible in helping my mother. But it is good for me to stop and remember that I am not God. I am not in the place of God. I am not an ever-present help. I am sinful. I will fail. I cannot control the present or foresee the future. All this territory belongs to God. He is the only one who can perfectly and actively help my parent—and who can help me.

Here is the needful truth for me as well: God is *my* ever-present help, as I, by his grace, help my aging loved one. I will be a better help to her if God is my present help, and if I trust God to be her help. Help comes from God; we just pass it on. This means I don't just need to read God's Word to my mother; I need to read God's Word and hear his voice myself. I don't just need to bring her into the fellowship of God's people; I need to be a regular part of that fellowship myself. I must be learning to trust God's help.

Help That Brings Good

To trust God's help for an aging person is to expect good from God. Not just basic survival, but *good*. His help is a redeeming help, help that brings light out of darkness. His help is an active help; what comfort to know that one greater than myself is always watching over my loved one (and me), night and day. Round-the-clock human help is so expensive; how amazing that we can call on the very power of heaven, provided for us richly in Christ. Hebrews tells us that believers can *confidently* say, "The Lord is my helper" (Heb. 13:6).

And heaven brings not just minimal assistance, as we expect in many "assisted-living" situations these days. Paul's affirmation of God's help is ultimately and overwhelmingly positive when he says that, although "our outer self is wasting away, our inner self is being renewed day by day" (2 Cor. 4:16). God's help brings *renewal*.

The Old Testament story of Caleb is remarkable. None of us can expect to repeat it exactly, but we can surely be encouraged by it. Caleb was forty years old when Moses sent him to spy out the promised land; of the twelve spies sent, only Caleb and Joshua came back urging the people to trust God and take the land despite its strong cities and its big, intimidating people called the "Anakim" (see Num. 13:25–33; Josh. 14:7). Forty-five years later, after Joshua has led the people in taking the land, Caleb comes to Joshua and says that he knows the Lord has kept him alive all these years, and he asks Joshua for the land Moses promised him:

> And now, behold, I am this day eighty-five years old. I am still as strong today as I was in the day that Moses sent me; my strength now is as my strength was then, for war and for going and coming. So now give me this hill country of which the LORD spoke on that day, for you heard on that day that the Anakim were there, with great fortified cities. It may be that the LORD will be with me, and I shall drive them out just as the LORD said. (Josh. 14:10–12)

Old Caleb is renewed both inwardly *and* outwardly! But he clearly understands that both kinds of strength are gifts from the Lord, which he eagerly accepts and according to which he humbly but optimistically sets his expectations: "It may be that the LORD will be with me, and I shall drive them out," says Caleb.

I don't know many eighty-five-year-olds who are as physically strong as Caleb seems to have been. But I know some who are as strong in their spirits, as the Holy Spirit clearly renews them day by day through their faith in Christ and his Word and through their participation in the family of God. God's Spirit is present and active in Christians of all ages and stages.

The prophet Joel gave us God's promise: "I will pour out my Spirit on all flesh; your sons and your daughters shall prophesy, your old men shall dream dreams, and your young men shall see visions" (Joel 2:28). Jesus promised his disciples that the "Helper," that is, the Holy Spirit, would come to guide and comfort and strengthen them after he rose from the dead and ascended to heaven (see John 16:7–15). At Pentecost, the Spirit of the risen Christ did come and indwell God's people in a new and full way (see Acts 2). His Spirit has always been at work in and among God's people, but we who live in these last days get to know God's help through the Spirit of the risen Christ, whom he sent to dwell within us until he comes again.

Through his Spirit God actively brings good in and through his people to the end of their earthly lives, as our inner selves are renewed day by day, to the very last day. In this way, God redeems the sufferings of old age. The Bible affirms the goodness of God's gift of life even into its later years—as evidenced by that beautiful recurring Old Testament phrase "a good old age."

God spoke to Abram (whom he later named Abraham) not only all the promises of blessing for the people who would come from his seed; he graciously gave him this promise as well: "As for you, you shall go to your fathers in peace; you shall be buried in a good old age" (Gen. 15:15). Indeed, Genesis 25:8 tells us that "Abraham breathed his last and died in a good old age, an old man and full of years, and was gathered to his people." King David likewise "died at a good age, full of days, riches, and honor" (1 Chron. 29:28).

The Bible's basic perspective is that life is a gift, for as long as God gives it, to the end. Wisdom, as it is personified in the book of Proverbs, holds "long life . . . in her right hand" as a blessed gift for those who listen to her (Prov. 3:16). Elsewhere, we read that "the fear of the LORD prolongs life" (Prov. 10:27)—and this long life is a good gift from God. We humans have no breath of life in ourselves: every breath we take is allowed and enabled by our Creator

God, for his perfect redemptive purposes. From this perspective, the purposeful termination of a human life by a means such as euthanasia looks even more evil and rebellious: how do we created beings dare to presume we should take the place of God in cutting off the breath of life that comes from him?

But how is one more day of pain and loneliness a good thing, a struggling aged person might well ask? I imagine many of us have known more than a few old and feeble people who wonder out loud just why God would keep them alive to suffer day by day. There is no easy answer to recite, but we might want to begin by reminding them that God is our help, our ever-present help in trouble. To know that help, through God's own Son, is a good and blessed thing. To bear witness to that help is a good thing; even angels are watching (see, for example, 1 Cor. 4:9). To spread that help, even just through a prayer, is a good and blessed thing. We might also want to talk about how God's help carries each life to its perfect completion.

Help That Completes

Christians can be sure that God's help perfectly covers the arc of our lives from beginning to end. God knows us from eternity past: he saw us being formed in the womb (see Ps. 139:15), and he chose us in Christ "before the foundation of the world" (Eph. 1:4). God ordains our future, not just our eternal future but also the precise future of our earthly existence, all the way up to the time of our death: again we turn to Psalm 139, where David affirms that God knows the exact number of our days, which were all written in his book before we were yet born (see Ps. 139:16). Even in the midst of persecution and imprisonment, the apostle Paul teaches that God's good hand shapes the entire span of a believer's existence: "I am sure of this, that he who began a good work in you will bring it to completion at the day of Jesus Christ" (Phil. 1:6).

For elderly people, how crucial to consider God's sovereign knowledge of the number of their days, the exact arc of their lives —and, in particular, the conclusion of that arc. If they do not know the Lord, this prospect makes knowing him the most urgent thing in the universe: meeting the Lord either through death or through Christ's return is not simply an abstract thought but a fast-approaching appointment.

Helping our loved ones prepare for that meeting is of prime importance. As we do our best, trust in God's sovereign goodness is the bedrock of our hope. If they do know the Lord, then what an amazing and comforting prospect, not just for our loved ones but for us who wait with them: to have confidence in God's perfect completion of the earthly life of his children—called home at just the right time, to be with him.

God's help is clearly and vividly promised for the closing portions of that arc. Interestingly, in passages that land on the promise of his care to the end, we often find an affirmation of his care from the beginning as well. This makes sense, for God's care in the final stages brings the *completion* of an entire life, one sovereignly designed by our Creator in his flawless plan. No one says it more beautifully than the prophet Isaiah, who brings us the very words of God:

> Listen to me, O house of Jacob,
> all the remnant of the house of Israel,
> who have been borne by me from before your birth,
> carried from the womb;
> even to your old age I am he,
> and to gray hairs I will carry you.
> I have made, and I will bear;
> I will carry and will save. (Isa. 46:3–4)

We often quote verse 4 to older folks, assuring them that God will watch over them even to old age and gray hairs. But look at these two verses together: What is the repeated word that connects them? It's the word *carry*. God doesn't just tell his children that he will carry them at the end; he says he carries them from the womb to old age—all the way, from the beginning to the end of our earthly lives. All the way my Savior leads me. All the way my Savior carries me.

Psalm 71 prays these truths back to God in a powerful way. Two passages make especially clear the psalmist's trust in God's help from beginning to end:

> For you, O Lord, are my hope,
> my trust, O Lord, *from my youth.*
> Upon you I have leaned *from before my birth*;
> you are he who took me *from my mother's womb.*
> My praise is continually of you.
>
> I have been as a portent to many,
> but you are my strong refuge.
> My mouth is filled with your praise,
> and with your glory all the day.
> Do not cast me off *in the time of old age*;
> forsake me not when my strength is spent. (vv. 5–9)
>
> O God, *from my youth* you have taught me,
> and I still proclaim your wondrous deeds.
> So *even to old age and gray hairs*,
> O God, do not forsake me,
> until I proclaim your might to another generation,
> your power to all those to come. (vv. 17–18)

The psalmist is teaching us how to trust in God from youth to old age (there's the gray hair again!). What stands out in this prayer is not just the confidence in God's overarching care but also the repeated desire to "praise" and "proclaim" God's "wondrous deeds" and "might" and "power" to the very last breath we have—and not just for ourselves, but for the generations that come after us.

This psalm centers on declaring God's marvelous salvation to the end. With his outward focus, the psalmist senses God's help sustaining not only his entire life but also the generations of lives that will finally complete the redeemed people of God. There is a bigger arc that shapes mine. Prayerfully focusing on the big story we're a part of helps us make our way faithfully to the ends of our own chapters.

Unfinished things leave us disturbed and dissatisfied. We humans long for completion. In an academic course, an "Incomplete" means we have not passed; we get no credit, for we have not finished. I always have a hard time going to bed before I'm finished writing a talk or preparing a document for the next day; I'm not able to rest until at least one full draft is complete. We know how we feel when the power goes out in the middle of watching a movie. Think of how desolate is the sight of a construction project that was begun and then abandoned; the skeleton frame and unfinished beams look forlorn and forsaken by the side of the road as we drive by.

We can sometimes fear that our lives will look incomplete at the end—and our loved ones may certainly battle such fears. Will we have finished all the work we were called to do? What have we built, and what does it look like as people drive by? Will the end be messy and chaotic, rather than beautiful and glorious? Will we go out as T. S. Eliot described in his poetic expression of the futility and hopelessness of modern existence: "This is the way the world ends . . . not with a bang but a whimper"?[1]

As we have seen, the Bible answers these questions about the completion of a life. The answers are found in the God who carries his people from the womb to old age, from birth to death. Each full chapter of each life is perfectly complete, for the God of our salvation is writing the story. He will help us to the end.

1. T. S. Eliot, "The Hollow Men," 1925.

Help through Prayer

All of that said, it can be hard to make our way through the closing passages of our individual chapters. The ending of most things is hard, especially when it comes at an unknown time. God knows the exact number of our days, but we do not—and so, as we age, we humans wait and wonder how and when the very end will come.

Death is the great mystery that will certainly unfold, but just how it will make its appearance we do not know. It might be sudden or quick. It might involve long, slow degeneration and suffering. We see examples of all kinds all around us all the time. Our aged loved ones are full of wondering, especially as they watch God reveal the ends of so many of their friends' earthly lives. One by one, these days, my mother's friends are gone, though no dates for their passing were set on her calendar.

We caregivers wait and wonder too, trying to organize our multifaceted lives around caring for our parents without having a known end point to work with. I recently spoke with a woman who told me all about how she and her husband brought his mother into their home so they could care for her during what they were told would be the final few weeks of her life . . . and a few weeks turned out to be a few years, upending their family's long-term plans in a big way (but also letting them learn God's grace in a bigger way than they had expected).

Psalm 71 (and all the psalms) points us to a kind of waiting that gives us access to God's help moment by moment. It is waiting filled with prayer. In the midst of so much that we cannot know, to know the one who knows all and who loves us infinitely is the greatest comfort. He is the one with the master calendar. In the end, there is nowhere else to go than to the God who carries us from the womb to old age.

The New Testament book of Hebrews shows us how we can go to him with confidence through his Son, our Great High Priest, who is able to sympathize with our weaknesses, for he "in every respect has been tempted as we are, yet without sin" (Heb. 4:15). Hebrews calls us to draw near to the throne of grace through Jesus Christ the Son of God, "that we may receive mercy and find grace to help in time of need" (v. 16).

Near the throne of grace, then, is where we find the help we need. We might think of Jesus himself in the days leading up to his crucifixion; he was not old, but he was nearing the end of his earthly life, and he needed grace to face that end—so he prayed to his Father in heaven. What a humbling example for us who are not without sin and who so often turn elsewhere for help. Jesus knew the details of the death that faced him as he prayed in the garden of Gethsemane; he was not praying to know, but rather asking his Father for help as he faced scorn and suffering and a shameful death on a cross. He understood not just the physical suffering but even more so the agonizing task of bearing our sin and suffering the wrath of God in our place. This was the "cup" Jesus prayed for his Father to remove, if his Father was willing—and then came the words of submission: "Nevertheless, not my will, but yours, be done" (Luke 22:42; see also Matt. 26:39).

Jesus the Son of God prayed for help as he embraced the completion of his life on earth—and the completion of the work of salvation he had come to accomplish. He knew the help that prayer would bring as he faced the suffering before him; in fact, he asked his closest disciples to pray with him—and his sleepy friends didn't do a very good job. Jesus went to pray not just once but three times that night in the garden; he knew prayer was a matter not of saying it and being done, but of communing with his Father and waiting in his Father's presence. It was a hard waiting as Jesus persevered in prayer: "Being in agony he prayed more earnestly; and his sweat became like great drops of blood falling down to the ground" (Luke 22:44).

And yet Luke tells us that an angel from heaven came and strengthened him. Jesus found real, active help from his Father as he faced death on a cross to save sinners like you and me. He went to the cross and accomplished that salvation. From the outside, it looked like a dreadful, incomplete ending. In God's eyes, though, it was complete. Jesus said, "It is finished," and then he "bowed his head and gave up his spirit" (John 19:30).

We can learn from Jesus. *Through* Jesus, who died for us, we can go to the throne of grace and find help in time of need. Because Jesus suffered God's wrath for us, our need will never be as deep as the need Jesus experienced in that garden; we believers face suffering and death, but by God's grace we are spared the wrath of judgment and hell, and we have the certain hope of eternal life that Jesus purchased for us through his blood.

The final big truth of this book will focus on that hope. But at this point, we must stop and affirm the help that leads us to the moment when the hope bursts into fulfillment. Yes, we will see Jesus and be with him, but the path leading to that moment is a path of walking in faith—and prayer—to the end.

Some aging people are saints who love to pray and who have cultivated the practice of prayer. What examples for us younger ones—often the busy, sleepy ones—who need to learn that practice of prayer both now and as we prepare ourselves for the final stages of our own lives, whatever they may be. But some aging people arrive at the end and have not practiced prayer, and so they struggle to go to God and find the help they need. We younger ones can help them find that help—and helping them will give us good practice ourselves.

This sort of practice is more urgent than most of us realize. I'm always convicted by Paul's description of a godly widow and wonder if I would be this kind of widow, should God choose to take my husband to heaven before me: "She who is truly a widow, left all alone, has set her hope on God and continues in supplications and prayers night and day" (1 Tim. 5:5). (We might remember the widow Anna, who worshipped "with fasting and prayer night and day"—Luke 2:37.) If we think this description is just one pleasant option, we need to read on to hear Paul's alternative: "She who is self-indulgent is dead even while she lives" (1 Tim 5:6).

It seems to me there is no better way to help an older person than by going with them to our heavenly Father and waiting in his presence, praising him for his marvelous works, claiming the promises of his Word, pleading for his grace for those around us (especially the next generations), and seeking his help for the path that lies ahead of us. We don't have to be experts in prayer—and aging loved ones are often the most patient and appreciative people we could ever find to pray with. We can pray the Psalms; they are the best teachers of the best kinds of prayers. And so, for our loved ones, we will be the kind of help that turns them to the best help of all, the help of God.

One of my favorite verses in the Bible comes from Proverbs and offers a picture of the life path of a redeemed child of God: "The path of the righteous is like the light of dawn, which shines brighter and brighter until full day" (Prov. 4:18). I hate driving at night in the dark. But I don't mind starting out at dawn when it is still dark, because I know the light will gradually break as the sun rises. And so is the path of the one made righteous by God's grace: that path does not get darker and darker as we head toward death.

Yes, every path travels through darkness in this fallen world. And, yes, we must say with grief that the path of one who does not know the Lord heads toward ultimate darkness and destruction rather than light. But we can say with confidence, on the authority of the Word of God, that the path of one who knows the Lord is brighter and brighter as we head toward the end—"brighter and brighter until full day." Our inner self is actually being renewed day by day. By the Spirit and the Word and the people of God, our spiritual eyes see better and better the invisible reality that is right there. We more and more confidently approach the throne of grace, and we find help that lights our way as we prepare to meet the One who is the light of the world.

Present help. Help that brings good. Help that completes. Help through prayer. O God, be the help of our dearly loved older ones, to the end. Be our help, we pray.

8

Responding with Faith

All our discussion so far has been leading us to respond to this fourth big truth of God's help to the end, help for our aging loved ones and for ourselves as we care for them. In response to a God who is sovereign over the aging process, who commands us to honor the aging, and who sees the sufferings of old age, we have discussed the three respective responses of humility, respect, and compassion—all responses that depend on God's help for us to live them out, and all responses that require the underlying response of faith. To seek and find God's help to the end, as humble, respectful, compassionate caregivers for our aging loved ones, what we most fundamentally need is faith.

The Bible defines faith as "the assurance of things hoped for, the conviction of things not seen" (Heb. 11:1). That definition is of infinite help in caring for elderly parents and loved ones, for the physical realities of aging bodies and minds would leave us desolate and helpless if they were all we had to work with. We need the invisible realities even more when the visible ones are painful and without an earthly cure.

These invisible realities are what we hear the apostle Paul affirm in that amazing claim to which we keep returning: that, "though our outer self is wasting away, our inner self is being renewed day by day" (2 Cor. 4:16). Paul made that claim by faith: he could not see the inner renewal with his physical eyes, but he believed in the reality of that renewal by faith—a faith not grounded in his own strength to believe, but a faith grounded in God's Son, revealed in God's Word, empowered through God's Spirit, and lived out among God's people.

What a gift from God, this faith in Christ Jesus. Faith begins as the Holy Spirit convicts our hearts of sin, and we respond by trusting in the saving work of Christ on our behalf, through his death on the cross and his resurrection from the dead. "For by grace you have been saved through faith. And this is not your own doing; it is the gift of God" (Eph. 2:8).

We can ask God for this gift of faith—just like the man who cried out to Jesus, "I believe; help my unbelief!" (Mark 9:24). And God is gracious to give us not only saving faith at the start, but growing faith all through our journey, as the invisible spiritual realities become more and more visible to our spiritual eyes—until the day when faith becomes sight, and we get to see him face-to-face.

By faith we seek and find the help of God as we point our loved ones to that help and as we depend on that help ourselves. Many of my friends who are also caring for aging loved ones agree that this caregiving process is one of the greatest and most challenging ways to grow in faith. The challenges are similar to those involved in raising children: we spend our prayers and efforts to help young people aim for not just visible but invisible success; we raise them to know and serve God forever. We're aiming to "fit them for heaven," just as we are with our aging parents. But with children, we most often get to see the physical growth along with the spiritual. With parents heading for death, what we most often see is physical decline, decline that, if we're not careful, can grow so large in our eyes as to obscure our spiritual vision—our faith.

By faith we seek and find the help of God; by faith we rest in the help of God; by faith we celebrate the help of God.

Faith That Seeks and Finds God's Help

Help is something that by its nature is passed on . . . given and received . . . sought and found. It ultimately comes from God, through his Word and by his Spirit, as we have seen. As we human beings receive God's help by faith, we pass it on in all sorts of ways —ways not measurable as in the passing on of money, but ways just as real and even more lasting. We pray for God's help for ourselves and others. We point others to God's help. We bear witness to God's help. We sing about it, often with others—just as the psalmists did. Seeking and finding God's help is an active process shared by faith and passed on generation by generation, in a multitude of ways.

Sometimes we caregivers get to see deep into an aging person's relationship with God; sometimes we don't. In some cases, after they are gone we find notes and journals that give us amazing glimpses into this relationship—like lamps that light up their lives for us and help urge us who come after them to keep moving toward the light. Through all kinds of examples, those who go before us help us on.

My mother-in-law was an unbelievably gracious but quite private person; our family, though, thinks she would not have minded the sharing of some of her written meditations found after her death, as her words offer great encouragement to those of us who will ourselves someday know the hardships of old age—perhaps even, as she experienced, the loss of a spouse. "Grandma Lo," as our children called Lois Nielson, truly found her help in God to the end; she went to be with the Lord at the age of ninety-one, on July 13, 2014, twelve years to the day following the death of her beloved husband, Robert Nielson ("Grandpa Bob"). The following words were written by Lois in longhand—we think about four years after her husband died. We found them in a drawer of her desk the day after her memorial service.

Since July 13, 2002, there have been many moments of an overwhelming sense of aloneness. They could not be relieved by activity or friends or family or tears.

We were husband and wife but also best friends. Bob's smile and love and energy had been a sustaining, comforting reality in my life for sixty-two years—that's three generations. Perhaps I supplied detail and facility, but he supplied delight and fragrance. He was a "let's do it" guy.

Often my bold front and forced smile were masking a heavy ache inside for the one I had loved dearly for those sixty-two years. The loss was sudden; God's timing seemed brutal.

As the lonely days slid, one by one, into a sort of hollow, "without Bob" routine, I was increasingly aware that grief has a bottom floor. The elevator can go no way but up.

I would not stay in the basement. With his usual zest, Bob would have said, "Let's go!"

Gathering my depleted resources, I pushed the button. Nothing happened. Of course not! The elevator needed power.

So I went again to the source which had supplied direction, power, and lift for every strategic crux and challenge since I was in college. I knew it well:

> Have you not known? Have you not heard?
> The LORD is the everlasting God,
>   the Creator of the ends of the earth.
> He does not faint or grow weary;
>   his understanding is unsearchable.
> He gives power to the faint,
>   and to him who has no might he increases strength.
> Even youths shall faint and be weary,
>   and young men shall fall exhausted;
> but they who wait for the LORD shall renew their strength;
>   they shall mount up with wings like eagles;

> they shall run and not be weary;
> they shall walk and not faint. (Isa. 40:28–31)
>
> Everything I needed was there: everlasting God . . . unsearchable understanding . . . power to the faint . . . wait for the Lord . . . renew strength . . . mount up with wings . . . walk and not faint.
>
> This time, for life's hardest moment, it was imperative to grasp the reality in those words of Isaiah.
>
> What a life support system! His presence, his promises undergirding and surrounding and uplifting. It is the real reality, the most tangible intangible resource on earth. It is ours for the asking, available without money or price, if we believe with our whole being.

It almost seems that Lois was reaching out in that last paragraph to share this help she found by faith, recommending that whoever reads her words would join her in believing God's promises "with our whole being." I know she prayed every day for her children, her grandchildren, and her great-grandchildren (some yet unborn!), that they would also walk and keep walking with faith in these promises. Generation by generation, we make our way by faith—and it helps immensely to find the reached-out hand of the generation that has gone before. They help us on.

Theologian and teacher D. A. Carson tells of such passed-on help in his book about his father.[1] One way Dr. Carson clearly honored him was to write this warm, wise account of his father Tom Carson's faithful Christian life as a pastor in Quebec, Canada. Toward the book's end, he includes some of the entries he found in

1. D. A. Carson, *Memoirs of an Ordinary Pastor: The Life and Reflections of Tom Carson* (Wheaton, IL: Crossway, 2008). The discussion of Tom Carson's last few years, including his journals, is found on pages 139–48.

his father's journals from the last few years of his life. Tom's wife had died, and he was still preaching now and then, but gradually weakening. In his journals he quoted much Scripture in Greek, French, and English, with often lengthy meditations and commentary. He quoted hymns and poetry, such as the following lines:

> *Wednesday, Apr. 6, 1992*
> My soul is night, my heart is steel,
> I cannot think, I cannot feel.
> For light and life I must appeal
> In simple faith to Jesus.

Appealing "in simple faith to Jesus": there is the key. Scattered throughout those journal pages were prayers of faith, such as "Keep me from the sins of old men," some of which Dr. Carson's father listed: "A tendency to gravitate toward watching television, the temptation to look backward instead of forward, sliding toward self-pity, easy resentment of young men." This elderly pastor wrote admonitions to himself, such as "Develop, as a senior, a prayer ministry: God has given you the time for it." Or "God had a plan to take Mum home and a plan to leave me here." And he wrote assurances of faith, affirming a "deepening experience of God" and a "heightened awareness that all of his acceptability before God turns on the gospel of the death and resurrection of Jesus Christ."

What a gift, such steady words of faith passed on. We do not all get to receive such help directly from our parents, but sharing words like these shares the help of these mothers and fathers in the faith—along with the stories of faithful believers down through the centuries. Such words from this great cloud of witnesses strengthen our faith and guide us in helping and praying for our aged loved ones as they approach the end of their journeys. Who knows what deep prayers and thoughts are percolating within those aging bodies, as the Spirit of God is at work like the invisible wind. Who knows what we might find later in their desk drawers or journals—or in their stories told in heaven.

Both my mother-in-law and Dr. Carson's father were putting their faith in what they could not see, as they walked in faith to the end. Lois aptly called the presence and the promises of God "the most tangible intangible resource on earth." And both clearly accessed that resource by seeking and finding help in the Word of God—which the Spirit used to strengthen and sustain them.

We must never underestimate the great extent to which we can help an aging person simply by sharing with them the Word of God—reading it aloud, listening with them to the reading and preaching of the Word, singing it in hymns and songs, referring to it in the course of our conversation and our prayers. The Word of God is alive and active, able to pierce a person's soul as the Holy Spirit drives it in deep and reveals the truths of Jesus on every page (see Heb. 4:12). Generation by generation, we can help pass it on.

Faith That Rests in God's Help

We who care for the elderly can pass on God's Word and God's help to them as clearly and lovingly as possible—but their response is not up to us; their souls are in the hands of God. What is up to us, with God's help, is *our* response in faith to God's Word.

This distinction (between their response and ours) is actually the first part of resting in God's help as we help our aging loved ones: because our good and gracious God is in charge of our parents' response, we can rest in his sovereign plan for them. As Jacob told Rachel, we humans are not in the place of God.

When we instruct young ones, we are, in a sense, in charge of their response, in that we must discipline them (as best we can) to hear and obey God's Word. We cannot control their heart response —which is also in God's hands—but we do to some extent control the process of children's listening and learning.

It is not the same with our parents. We do not discipline them, for they are not our children. Rather, we honor them to the end by respecting them as the parents given to us by the Lord. We help them as fully as possible—and we leave their response to God's Word in God's good hands. They belong to him.

Many an adult child among my acquaintances is worried and upset by an elderly parent who is unhappy, discontent, and bitter (maybe even toward their child) concerning the hardship and the loneliness of his or her final years. Now, this discussion assumes that the adult child is loving and caring for his or her parent as well as possible, aiming for the kind of respect and compassion and help we are setting forth in this book. As we have said, no child or caregiver will do it perfectly. We will often fail. But we are talking here about one who wholeheartedly aims to give good and loving care, by God's grace.

For such a faithful one, it is important to say that the results are not always happy. The sad truth is that even the best, most faithful caregiver cannot fix all the pain and isolation and suffering of an aging loved one—and sometimes all that unfixable distress just overflows onto the caregiver. It makes sense that this would be so, for the caregiver is right there, probably the closest available receptacle for that poured-out unhappiness. We aim to help our aging parents find their help in God in the midst of trouble, but sometimes they turn instead only to us—to us who are not God.

Just as we must ultimately learn to give up our children into God's hands, so we must learn to give up our parents. As we continue to help, we will still suffer with them in their pain, but we must not take their anger or bitterness or discontent into our souls such that we share those qualities or let our thoughts be flavored with them. By faith we can trust the Lord God, whose hand is on our parents—and us. We cannot see him, but we know he is there. He is there as we listen to our loved ones, as we come alongside them, and as we pray. We can hold our struggling parents with open hands before our sovereign, compassionate God, asking him and trusting him to work in their souls. We can give them up to him.

And then we can rest, both spiritually and physically, no matter what our parents' response. Our Shepherd can handle all within his great flock; we are just one of the sheep. We can pray in faith with the psalmist, "In peace I will both lie down and sleep; for you alone, O Lord, make me dwell in safety" (Ps. 4:8). And we can awake with thanksgiving and praises and petitions, for, through Christ our Great High Priest, we can confidently approach the throne of heaven and find help in time of need. We can minister with clear hearts in multiple directions—to other family members, and church members, and friends and coworkers; our worlds are bigger than our parents, even though caring for them can sometimes seem all-consuming. We can ask others to pray with us, especially for a hurting parent. In all these things we can confidently say, by faith, "The Lord is my helper" (Heb. 13:6).

This is not easy. Caregiving is not a onetime occasion we can rise to and then recover from; it is more often like a long path with no clear end. Seeking and finding God's help is a growing walk of faith; we keep learning, day by day. But praise God that we keep learning day by day—and, we recall, the Word tells us that our path is like the first gleam of dawn, shining ever brighter until the full light of day. There is light, and there is rest, on this path of faith in the Lord Jesus.

Of course, many parents are just the opposite of unhappy and discontent. I have one friend who cares full-time for her mother and who has told me multiple times, "I want to be just like my mother when I am old!" Now there is a goal to aim for: that our children or those caring for us would someday say those words! I would guess that most parents are sometimes one way, sometimes another. It helps to remember again and again just how we children of the heavenly Father must appear to him—sinful and changeable as we are. He hears all our complaints, and he works in our souls to turn our bitterness and discontent into thanksgiving and praise. He helps us. Once he has made us his children, with hearts cleansed by faith in the blood of Christ shed for us, he never turns his back on us: we are his sheep, and he will bring us all the way home.

One last thing about sheep: they live in flocks. Each one knows the shepherd's voice (see John 10:4), but together the sheep feed, and follow, and rest. We caregivers must keep remembering that we are not meant to do this work alone; we need all kinds of help. God helps his children through his Word and by his Spirit, but he means us to receive that help as part of his people, members of the body of Christ . . . sheep, led by one Shepherd. We need the prayers and, sometimes, the hands and feet of brothers and sisters in that body, and we should humbly ask for that help and receive it with thanksgiving.

If our family members are part of the body of Christ, it is a special joy to pray for and love and serve our aging loved ones together; if not, we can still learn with joy to help one another well in our caregiving—and we believers can lead the way by showing Christ's love. In any case, we are all called to care well for the spiritual mothers and fathers of our church body; some of the aging sheep (or the struggling caregivers) may be alone in this world and may desperately need the flock.

God often sends help to caregivers in surprising ways, sometimes when we feel most alone. We can pray for eyes of faith to see and receive that help with thankful hearts. During my mother's complicated series of hip surgeries last year, the hours of watching by her hospital bedside often stretched long, and I broke them up with periodic walks around the floor—during which I encountered various nurses and aides. One young aide was especially open to chatting, and I stopped one afternoon to talk with her, hoping for a chance to discuss spiritual things. As it turned out, she began to ask me questions. . . . Where was I from? . . . Did I have family members near or far? And so forth. I think I must have looked tired.

Before I had a chance to try to encourage her or know her better, she stopped, looked me in the eye, and said, "You know, you are here because God put you here. God never puts you anywhere by mistake." And then she smiled and was off down the hall. What a gift were her words. Who knows . . . maybe she was an angel.

Faith That Celebrates God's Help

If I'm looking for topics of conversation with Mom that will take our attention off immediate hurts or frustrations, it often helps to ask her about God's help in the past—to open some of the happy chapters of her life story. Of course, we have to take care: there will be sad chapters that we're better off not bringing to mind. In our case, for example, I would not delve into the years of my father's or my sister's suffering before their deaths. But I *would* go further back: my mother has many joyful and fun memories of her courtship years with Dad. They were both engaged to others before they met, and their relationship was in process when they both participated in the wedding of his older brother to her older sister . . . it's a narrative with some pretty engrossing twists and turns.

Mom livens up when she relives memories from her years teaching in schools and directing music programs, from an amazing number of friendships that stretched into lifelong relationships (still producing mounds of annual story-stimulating Christmas and birthday cards), from family birthday and holiday celebrations that marked off the years with our favorite strawberry cake and butter cookies and corn puddings and slow-cooked beef brisket. Sometimes it takes just one leading question (sometimes more), and the floodgates of her memory open in a wonderful way. Often reliving such memories provides an opportunity to express appreciation for all that Mom did during those years: all the classes of children taught, all the choirs directed well, all the special *and* ordinary meals cooked, all the family faithfully loved . . .

It's almost always evident how much it means to recount these kinds of memories with an aging person. They are this person's treasures from the past, meant to be brought out and savored as, by faith, we see and celebrate God's help all along the way. When my mother moved from her independent apartment to her assisted-living one, it was sad to have to give so many things away. That's a huge understatement—although I was surprised by the composure with which Mom accepted the change. She knew it had to happen, she truly welcomed the greater help, and she set about planning the new space with as many treasures as we could fit in! Mom's acceptance was a gift to me, and we managed the move quickly and efficiently.

One thing that helped was to set aside some treasures. We kept a few special things (jewelry, pictures, decorative pieces) for each grandchild and put them all in what we call the "treasure box," which is now in her storage unit, to be opened after she dies. She had a whole shelf of teacups collected from various places and parts of her past: she called in friends and gave most of them away as gifts, one by one, telling their stories in the process. "This one came from Niagara Falls; we bought it on our honeymoon trip . . ."

Calling up such memories is a concrete way to celebrate the goodness of God, who has been our help through all our years. Many such memories are common grace, owned and shared by believers and nonbelievers alike, but all of them are gifts from the God who is the source of every good and gracious gift—and it sustains our souls to acknowledge that source. It strengthens our faith to see and say what God has done. God has been our help in ages past, in all things.

As we pray with our parents, it helps to thank God not just for the big gifts of salvation in Christ and the hope of heaven, but also for the little gifts through which the Lord provides: a pleasing meal, a memorable family outing, a safe trip, an enjoyable phone call from a friend, a day without a crisis. The more we grow eyes of faith in our God, who sovereignly superintends our lives from beginning to end, the more we see how he upholds our lives moment by moment. Indeed, he helps us like a loving father helps his child along a winding path, one that has some rough patches but also some smooth stretches with pleasant stopping points and great views—from our youth to old age and gray hairs.

One of our family's favorite hymns is "Come, Thou Fount of Every Blessing," a hymn of praise celebrating the merciful blessings of God toward his people.[2] The words were originally written in the eighteenth century by Robert Robinson, who was a difficult youth sent by his mother to London as a barber's apprentice but who, at age nineteen, heard a sermon by the preacher George Whitefield, was converted, and became a minister—a minister who wrote poems.

The hymn's second verse refers to 1 Samuel 7, a chapter that tells of how God answered the prophet Samuel's prayers for his people by defeating the enemy Philistine army—after which Samuel "took a stone and set it up between Mizpah and Shen and called its name Ebenezer; for he said, 'Till now the LORD has helped us'" (7:12). In the original Hebrew, "Ebenezer" literally means "stone of help." Verse two of our much-loved hymn begins:

> Here I raise my Ebenezer; hither by thy help I'm come;
> And I hope, by thy good pleasure, safely to arrive at home.

Generation after generation, God's people need to sing and celebrate God's help, all along the path and all the way home.

The greatest reason for celebration is the greatest help given to us by God: the gift of his saving grace toward us in Christ, received by faith. Robinson's hymn makes this clear in the final verse:

2. For more on this hymn, see Leland Ryken, *40 Favorite Hymns on the Christian Life: A Closer Look at Their Spiritual and Poetic Meaning* (Phillipsburg, NJ: P&R Publishing, 2019), 57–60.

O to grace how great a debtor daily I'm constrained to be;
Let that grace now, like a fetter, bind my wand'ring heart to thee.
Prone to wander, Lord, I feel it, prone to leave the God I love;
Here's my heart, O take and seal it, seal it for thy courts above.

By faith we see and celebrate the wonder of this grace poured out on us in Jesus Christ our Savior. Truly, by faith we seek and find the help of God in Christ; by faith we rest in the help of God in Christ; by faith we celebrate the help of God in Christ.

All the little gifts and helps sent by God are meant to point us to the greatest one, this unending help that lets us live and sing God's praises not just here but in the very presence of Jesus, and not just now but for eternity.

And that leads us to the subject of this book's final chapters.

9

God Reveals What Is to Come

This book could not be written without the fifth and final big biblical truth, one that lights up all the others. We considered first God's sovereign hand in aging—and our response of humility before our Creator. Second, we considered God's call to honor the aged—and our response of respect for our elders. Third, we considered God's eyes for the sufferings of old age—and our response of godly compassion. Fourth, we considered God's help to the end—and our response of faith in that unending help.

But the "end" we considered is an end with another side; death is the end to this earthly life, but it is the doorway into eternal life. We cannot see the other side of the doorway now, of course—which is why that response of *faith* is so important, to develop our eyesight for the eternal things we are about to see when we die or when Jesus returns, if he should return before our death.

For those who have received the gift of faith in Christ, physical death will mean immediately being "at home with the Lord," as Paul puts it. It is worth reading this phrase in context, for Paul shows the need for faith now as we prepare for the full reality then:

> So we are always of good courage. We know that while we are at home in the body we are away from the Lord, for we walk by

> faith, not by sight. Yes, we are of good courage, and we would rather be away from the body and at home with the Lord. So whether we are at home or away, we make it our aim to please him. For we must all appear before the judgment seat of Christ, so that each one may receive what is due for what he has done in the body, whether good or evil. (2 Cor. 5:6–10)

These are mysteries far beyond us, but they are mysteries revealed in God's inspired Word to light the way to the end and beyond. Paul is writing these words to believers in Jesus Christ, those who are aiming to meet the Savior who died for them, who rose from the dead, and who is seated now at the right hand of God the Father until that day when he will come again to the earth in all his glory to judge the living and the dead. This fifth truth is a stunning one: God actually tells us what is to come.

In light of this revelation, we must be struck again by the urgency of sharing Jesus Christ with those who have not put their faith in him. They will be there when we all appear before the judgment seat of Christ; every eye will finally see him (see Rev. 1:7), and every knee will bow (see Phil. 2:10). There is nothing more pressing in the world than preparing to meet Christ face-to-face. There is no greater gift we can give our aging loved ones than to point them to the truths of salvation revealed in God's Word. These truths help us here on earth, and they point the way home . . . to our eternal home, with the Lord Jesus.

This final big biblical truth takes us back to the first one we considered: even as we feel the urgency of sharing Jesus Christ with our loved ones in light of God's revelation of things to come, we remember again the sovereignty of our God who oversees the human story—and each human story. We can declare these truths about eternity, but it is the eternal God who is in charge. It is God who is all-powerful and only good. He is God, and we are not. We can trust his perfect purposes, from eternity past into eternity future. We can and must entrust our loved ones into his sovereign hands.

But let us speak these eternal realities, and speak them out loud, as God gives us opportunity. In this chapter, we will consider God's revelation about this eternal home with Jesus and what it means for us to help usher our loved ones into eternity.

A Faithful Usher's Certainty

The picture of an usher is not a bad one for those of us who help our aging parents or loved ones toward death and see them through the final stages. An ushering job is a humble one, for an usher disappears into the background: the focus is the person being ushered, and the one whom that person is being ushered in to see.

We might imagine a person being ushered into a royal throne room—or perhaps into the famous drawing room in Buckingham Palace: the usher opens the door from the hallway at the appointed time and allows the ushered one to go in, usually announcing his or her entrance. Often, however, ushers don't enter themselves; they just close the door quietly behind the person permitted to enter. An usher in a dark theater holds a flashlight and shows the doorway for the ones who get to enter the VIP box.

We ushers do not get to enter yet ourselves. But we need to know the way and hold the flashlight steady for the important ones who have these appointments made by God, with God. Many people around us will say we cannot be certain about life after death —or they will express their own subjective certainties: perhaps that everyone will share in some vague happy heaven with a tolerant Santa-Claus sort of god; perhaps that there will be no consciousness; perhaps that we will begin another life in some other form; perhaps that we can simply trust the goodness of nature to deal kindly and gently with us. Our natural human instinct is to hope for the best, even as our natural human fears (often unspoken) worry us, for most of us know deep down that we have not done our absolute best and may deserve the worst.

The beauty of Christian truth revealed by God himself in the Scriptures is that it acknowledges and deals with our worst fears: we *are* sinful creatures, ever since the fall of Adam and Eve—and we do deserve the worst. "The wages of sin is death" (Rom. 6:23). That death is both physical and spiritual. The good news comes in the rest of that same verse: "But the free gift of God is eternal life in Christ Jesus our Lord." On the cross, the sinless Christ bore our sins and suffered death for us—both physical and spiritual death. He suffered the very wrath of God that is hell, as punishment for our sin. And then he rose from the dead, conquering sin and death. Through faith in his saving work on our behalf, we are given his righteousness, and we receive the free gift of eternal life rather than eternal death. We can live and die expecting to meet the Savior who died for us.

These are the certain truths that a Christian "usher" knows; I am calling this usher a "faithful usher" because he or she has faith in the Lord Jesus Christ as revealed in his Word. Ushers without this faith can do a good job of helping an aging and dying person; whether they are believers or not, trained hospice caregivers, for example, often offer immense comfort to the dying as well as encouragement to the surrounding family. They know and practice the most effective methods of pain control, and they usually administer help with a straightforwardness and calm that many of my friends and I have noted with deep appreciation. Once a person has come to the point of hospice care or some equivalent, it is usually easier to talk openly about the process of dying, even if dying is not quite imminent. Caregivers experienced in this final stage of life can play a huge part in helping with those conversations, and with the practical details of bodies shutting down and accepting less or no food, and so forth. We should embrace the help of those acquainted with these hard details.

But such caregivers are not usually trained to be ushers into the presence of Jesus. They can help a person down the hall, but some of them have and some of them don't have the flashlight to light up the doorway. What a mercy that God has illumined the doorway for us in the Scriptures. We might think of Revelation 4, where, in a vision from God, the apostle John was actually allowed to see "a door standing open in heaven!" (v. 1). In his vision, John was called to enter that door and to gaze upon heaven with its throne —and, most importantly, the One seated on that throne. John witnesses the glorious heavenly celebration of redemptive history, with Jesus the Lamb of God standing at the center, worshipped by all the hosts of heaven. He is the spotless sacrifice who was slain to ransom his people "from every tribe and language and people and nation" (Rev. 5:9).

The point here is not to study these heavenly realities in detail, but rather to affirm that they are real, right there beyond the door. We can be certain; we have God's Word on it. How gracious for him to reveal these truths to us, so that we can walk toward them with a sure faith. The job of an usher is to help a dying person walk through that door, trusting the God who will burst into sight on the other side.

For those of us who belong in faith to the Lord Jesus, the place beyond the door is home. By the time we get there, we will have longed for that place, where we will see Jesus. We will have realized that we don't fully fit or truly settle in any other home along the way. We will have known that our true citizenship is in heaven with him (see Phil. 3:20).

The wonder of an usher is that we get to affirm these truths by faith—and, even as we affirm them, we grow in our faith. We have been given the flashlight, we know the way to the door, and we believe even if we haven't yet seen for ourselves what is beyond it. Our spiritual eyes become a little sharper as we peer with our loved ones into heaven. We read the old, old story of Jesus again and again, and it penetrates our hearts more and more deeply. We better understand the truth of what Jesus told that criminal hanging next to him who acknowledged him as king: "Truly, I say to you, today you will be with me in paradise" (Luke 23:43). It's not a long trip after a believer steps through that doorway. Heaven is right there. To be absent from the body is to be—immediately, *today*—home with the Lord.

A Faithful Usher's Expectations

The Bible does give us some details about what happens after we die; it is important for us ushers to speak with wisdom and certainty about what is revealed and with restraint about what is not. Along with certainty about a dying believer's immediate destination—home in heaven with the Lord Jesus—we can have some clear expectations about the unfolding of human history to the end.

As we have said, our little human stories are part of God's big redemptive story; after death, we expect to be part of God's perfect plan for the world he created and rules. That plan is centered on his Son, who came to redeem us and all of creation. For its completion, the plan awaits the second coming of Jesus to this earth—this time not as a baby but in glory, to judge all and to reign in a new heavens and a new earth.

When we believers die, then, we go to be with Jesus, but we, along with all creation, will be awaiting the final part of the story, when Jesus comes to earth again. Scripture tells us that not until Christ's return will bodies be resurrected; our bodies will remain in the grave and decay until that promised resurrection, when all will rise, "some to everlasting life, and some to shame and everlasting contempt" (Dan. 12:2; see also John 5:28–29). Looking forward to the end of earthly history gives us clear perspective on the time in which we now live—a time of God's mercy, when the gospel is preached and people are called to repent, and a time of his patience: God is patient, the Bible says, "not wishing that any should perish, but that all should reach repentance" (2 Peter 3:9).

In the meantime, during this period of mercy and patience, God will not lose track of all the bodies of those who have died, whether they are buried or lost at sea or burned or otherwise destroyed; he promises that those very bodies will be resurrected. Jesus, we know, was the first to be resurrected from the grave with a spiritual body that will never die. The apostle Paul calls Jesus the "firstfruits," explaining that, at his second coming, all believers will follow him (see 1 Cor. 15:22–23), rising from the dead just as he did, with bodies made new. Oh, what a prospect, especially after the process of aging, with all its degeneration: the prospect of a body made new. Paul offers a magnificent description of that final resurrection:

> Behold! I tell you a mystery. We shall not all sleep, but we shall all be changed, in a moment, in the twinkling of an eye, at the last trumpet. For the trumpet will sound, and the dead will be raised imperishable, and we shall be changed. For this perishable body must put on the imperishable, and this mortal body must put on immortality. When the perishable puts on the imperishable, and the mortal puts on immortality, then shall come to pass the saying that is written:
>
> "Death is swallowed up in victory."
> "O death, where is your victory?
> O death, where is your sting?" (1 Cor. 15:51–55)

God's purposes from creation will not be thwarted: his redeemed people will live forever with the Lord in bodies (perfect new bodies) on the earth (a new heaven and a new earth), all through the redeeming work of Jesus Christ. Through his Son, God makes *all* things new:

> For in him all the fullness of God was pleased to dwell, and through him to reconcile to himself all things, whether on earth or in heaven, making peace by the blood of his cross. (Col. 1:19–20)

What will this new, fully reconciled creation in Christ look like? What will our new bodies look like? Paul tells us to imagine putting a seed in the ground: "What is sown is perishable; what is raised is imperishable. . . . It is sown a natural body; it is raised a spiritual body" (1 Cor. 15:42, 44). The picture helps, but in truth we don't know exactly what those resurrected spiritual bodies will look like. We know we will be like Christ our risen Savior, and we will be with him, forever. The verse that affirms our citizenship in heaven continues,

> . . . from it we await a Savior, the Lord Jesus Christ, who will transform our lowly body to be like his glorious body, by the power that enables him even to subject all things to himself. (Phil. 3:20–21)

Until this promised day of resurrection, what should we expect? We've seen what happens to our bodies. What should we anticipate for the heavenly state of believers immediately after we die? Our spirits (our full, conscious, distinguishable selves, but without the ultimate fullness of our flesh) will be in heaven with Christ . . . what will that look like? Paul tries to imagine this state of waiting in heaven, this state that is perfect but incomplete (see 2 Cor. 5:2–8). He longs for it, because he knows he will be with his Savior, but he lets us in on his wonderings about it. He speaks of putting off this earthly "tent" (v. 4), this body in which we suffer and groan—and he trusts (almost with a smile, it seems) that he will not then be "naked" or "unclothed" (vv. 3–4). Indeed, he longs to be "further clothed, so that what is mortal may be swallowed up by life" (v. 4).

But here's where he lands: he affirms that it is God himself who has perfectly prepared us for all that is to come and who has given us his Spirit now as a guarantee . . . and so we can be of "good courage" (v. 8). This is the most basic truth, and it's all we really need to know: to be "away from the body" is to be "at home with the Lord" (v. 8). To be at home with Jesus in heaven after we die will be all good, very good.

We have lots of ideas about heaven in our minds, many of them inspired not by the Bible but by popular pictures and stories. In their clear, helpful book *If I Should Die Before I Wake*, K. Scott Oliphint and Sinclair B. Ferguson tell of hearing a radio program in which some famous people were interviewed about what they thought heaven would be like. The authors say they noticed three things:

1. All those interviewed believed in heaven.
2. All those interviewed assumed they would be there.
3. When asked to describe heaven, not one of those interviewed mentioned that God was there.[1]

How sad—but how common a perspective. In discussing heaven, people often talk about reuniting with family members who have died, or being able to do all their favorite activities, or enjoying places of beauty and peace. Surely there will be all kinds of joy in heaven, including the wonderful joy of being united with all God's family who have gone before us.

When the Bible depicts heaven, however, God and his throne are the center of attention. Heaven is heaven because it is where God dwells, our God in three persons who made and rules the world redeemed through his Son. Heaven will come down to earth one day,

1. K. Scott Oliphint and Sinclair B. Ferguson, *If I Should Die before I Wake: Help for Those Who Hope for Heaven* (Grand Rapids: Baker Books, 1995), 44.

when Jesus comes again: God will dwell among us, as he intended from the beginning (see Rev. 21:1–3). Until then, we his people get to dwell with him in heaven when we die. Awaiting these realities now, we can learn to pray with the psalmist, "Whom have I in heaven but you? And there is nothing on earth that I desire besides you" (Ps. 73:25).

Expectations are important. The Bible teaches us how to set expectations for what is to come after death—humbly but clearly, and all with a central focus on the Lord Jesus Christ. As we usher our loved ones toward death, and toward eternal life, we can help set expectations that are firmly grounded in God's Word. We can help point the way clearly toward our home with the Lord.

A Faithful Usher's Work

We ushers may be certain of the Bible's promises about our home in heaven with Jesus; the loved ones for whom we care may know and believe them as well; we may have our expectations clearly set for heaven and the final resurrection to come . . . and, still, crossing into eternal life may be hard. Christians are not promised a glorious death, even though we are promised glory immediately after death. Sometimes a Christian dies with joy and triumph; sometimes a Christian dies with calm or just quiet; sometimes a Christian dies with agonizing pain and fear.

We should not pretend that death is not a great enemy, even though it has already been defeated by Jesus Christ. We are still waiting for the final demise of death. One of the great scenes in the book of Revelation is the scene of final judgment before God's throne—specifically the moment when Death and Hades are thrown into the lake of fire forever (see Rev. 20:14). In the end, death will have no more sway.

In this present fallen world, though, we believers must still face the physical ravages of death. We know that death cannot separate us from the love of God in Christ Jesus our Lord (see Rom 8:38–39). But we still have to walk through the door.

The seventeenth-century English writer John Bunyan did not use the picture of a door; instead, he gave us that marvelous final scene in *The Pilgrim's Progress*, where Christian and his companion Hopeful approach the end of their long journey and must cross a very deep river to get to that shining city they can see on the other side. There is work to be done in the crossing, here at the journey's end. The two gold-clad angels who have come to escort them tell them, "You must go through, or you cannot come at the gate."[2]

This is really one of the hardest and most encouraging scenes in all of literature, I think, for Bunyan did not make that river a small thing. It is a hard, deep passage. Christian and Hopeful ask if there is another way to the gate, but the angels tell them that none except Enoch and Elijah have ever been permitted to use that other way. "Then they addressed themselves to the water, and entering, Christian began to sink, and crying out to his good friend Hopeful, he said, I sink in deep waters; the billows go over my head; all his waves go over me."[3]

You must read the entire scene for yourself. Hopeful tells Christian he feels the bottom, and it is good. But Christian's experience is different: he is full of fear, doubts about his sins, terror of evil spirits, and on and on . . . and Hopeful can barely keep Christian's head above water. But finally, Christian hears the psalms Hopeful keeps speaking to him, along with these simple words: "Be of good cheer, Jesus Christ maketh thee whole." "And with that Christian brake out with a loud voice, Oh, I see him again; and he tells me, 'When thou passest through the waters, I will be with thee; and through the rivers, they shall not overflow thee.' Isa. 43:2. Then they both

2. John Bunyan, *The Pilgrim's Progress from This World to That Which Is to Come* (Philadelphia: Porter & Coates, 1893), 235.

3. Bunyan, 235.

took courage, and the enemy was after that as still as a stone, until they were gone over."[4] And there are the shining ones waiting on the other side, ready to lead them right up to the gate of the city and into the presence of its King. They have passed through the waters, depending on Christ and not on themselves.

Our faith is measured not by anything in us but only by the object of our faith: as Hopeful said, it is Jesus Christ who makes us whole. We believers need not fear. We need not fear even our own fears—and some will have more of them than others. Our passings will unfold in all sorts of ways. But even in fearful passings, with Christ as our Lord we will cross over and be at home with him. Death cannot separate us from the love of God in Christ Jesus.

The work of a faithful usher can be compared to the work of Hopeful. Sometimes it is glorious work, even in the midst of sorrow. Sometimes it is agonizing work, in the midst of great pain and fear. It is the work of pointing a soul to the Lord Jesus in every way we can, particularly through speaking God's Word, which reveals truly what is to come and which comforts us in our fears along the way.

We ushers are not without help. The Holy Spirit is always at work, and we can trust the Spirit to take God's Word and make it bear fruit as God wills, even to the end, and sometimes in ways we cannot see on this side of heaven. God's Word will not return to him void; it will succeed exactly as God intends (see Isa. 55:11). We can read and speak that Word with faith, even when we feel we are sending out the words blindly; God will give them aim and efficacy.

On the day my father died, I had the great joy of being with him and my mother. We did not know he would go to heaven that day, although he was in hospice care and we knew his heart was failing fast—but my father had a way of coming through crisis after crisis with surprising resiliency. He had sat up for a while in a recliner that morning but then wanted to lie down, there in the skilled care unit

4. Bunyan, 237–38.

of the retirement community where he had lived and ministered to so many. He was known and loved, by residents and staff alike.

I asked if he would like me to read from the Bible; when he said yes, I turned to a passage I was working on for a conference talk—and he smiled when I told him so. He was invariably encouraging and interested in everything I ever worked on, and he was no different in his last hours. Even when medicated by morphine for his pain, he still responded lovingly. He and Mom read me the Word in my childhood; I got to read him the Word in his dying.

In God's providence, then, I turned to 1 Peter 1 and read verses 3–9, which are all about the blessing of being "born again to a living hope through the resurrection of Jesus Christ from the dead, to an inheritance that is imperishable, undefiled, and unfading, kept in heaven for you" (vv. 3–4). We could tell Dad was listening to every word. Later that day, when he suddenly sat up, raised both his arms, and took his last breath, Mom and I knew that he had entered heaven.

We have heaven's help in our work as ushers. We will not do it perfectly. Maybe we won't even get to be there—which gives us all the more reason to leave God's Word and God's promises echoing in the air whenever we leave an aged loved one's presence. But we can rest in the Lord, who sovereignly oversees every moment to the end.

And then there are the angels. We don't know too much about them, and it's best for our thoughts to be filled with Jesus instead. But the angels are all around us, these "ministering spirits sent out to serve for the sake of those who are to inherit salvation" (Heb. 1:14). In Jesus's story of the rich man and Lazarus, the poor man, Lazarus, died and "was carried by the angels to Abraham's side" (Luke 16:22). Maybe John Bunyan got it right, with those shining figures sent by God to escort Christian and Hopeful through the final portion of their journey home. Without a doubt, we have heaven's help in our ushering.

What a privilege to serve as a lowly usher for such a crossing—into the presence of Jesus. On the sure foundation of God's revelation, we can be ushers who have certainty about God's promises of eternal life with him. We can be ushers who have biblical expectations, expressed humbly but clearly, concerning the resurrection life that is our inheritance in Christ. We can be ushers who are unafraid to help our loved ones through that doorway—or across that river—no matter how great their (or our) sufferings and fears.

We ushers don't have to figure out this job ourselves; we have a perfect handbook sent from heaven. We have God's clear revelation of what is to come. How should we respond? We should respond with hope—biblical hope, eternal hope. Even in the face of death, we should respond, as Peter said, with "a living hope through the resurrection of Jesus Christ from the dead" (1 Peter 1:3). The final chapter will explore what it looks like to take after Bunyan's Hopeful —as we respond to God's revelation with true hope.

10

Responding with Hope

Let's let hope illumine the end of this book about caring for our aging loved ones. The forward pull of hope is our natural heart response to God's revelation of the good things to come. Indeed, hope should light up all our responses to the big biblical truths about aging that we have discussed.

There is great hope in the first truth we considered, the truth of God's sovereign hand in the process of aging and death. We need neither minimize nor fear these painful results of the fall that have come to all of us from the God who is sovereignly working out his redemptive plan in human history. We can humbly accept this truth with hope in God's good plan.

There is great hope in the truth of God's call to honor our parents and elders. This call turns our eyes and hearts toward our Father in heaven, the source of all life and our only hope in this life and the next. We can respect our earthly fathers and mothers with ultimate hope in our heavenly Father, who will bring us home to him.

There is great hope in the truth of God's eyes for the distinct sufferings of old age. We are not left alone to despair, either in our suffering or in our care for those who suffer, as God sees and cares for every inch of his creation. We can show compassion as we hope in our compassionate, redeeming God.

There is great hope in the truth of God's help to the end: God's Word assures his people of his presence even to old age and gray hairs, and that presence brings spiritual renewal along the path toward heaven. We can respond in faith that is fed by the hope of God's ever-present help every step of the way.

Finally, there is great hope in the truth of God's revelation of what is to come: even as we realize that this life will end, often with suffering, we can trust and share God's promises for God's people about heaven and resurrection life in his presence. We can respond with the sure hope of our everlasting home with the Lord.

Hope that characterizes the people of God is not a vague sort of optimism, but a certain assurance of God's eternal promises according to his inspired Word. Such a hope increasingly sets us apart in a world full of hopelessness. Many people in our time are consumed with fear about looming worldwide crises, whether through deadly pandemics, nuclear bombs, global warming, AI takeovers, or other catastrophic events. Many young couples all over the world are choosing not to have children, for a variety of reasons but often because they are afraid; such choices reflect, among other things, a pervasive hopelessness about the future and about God. According to the Centers for Disease Control and Prevention, suicide rates in the United States have increased by over 30 percent since 2000. In the year 2021 alone, 48,183 Americans died by suicide. The highest rates are among those eighty-five years and older.[1]

The world around us desperately needs hope; it is a matter not just of quality of life, but of life and death. As the elderly portion of the population steadily increases, and as the younger portion of caregivers steadily decreases, Christians have a distinct and growing

1. "Suicide Data and Statistics," Centers for Disease Control and Prevention, accessed December 5, 2023, https://www.cdc.gov/suicide/suicide-data-statistics.html.

opportunity to show hope in the face of both life and death. In particular, we believers, who trust God's revelation of what is to come after death, can bear witness to true hope as we help usher the dying into eternity. We can show and share hope that gives light, hope that energizes, and hope that grows.

Hope That Gives Light

Hope is the light of our expectations. Hope illumines what is invisible or dark ahead of us, so that we can assuredly walk toward the promise of good things. We have considered the truth of God's revelation concerning life after death. We have heard the promise for believers of a home in heaven with Christ and eternal life in the new heaven and the new earth with all God's redeemed people. Hope lets those truths light the way ahead.

For loved ones who are quickly approaching the end of their earthly lives, at what we might think of as the darkest point we can show them the brightest light, that is, Christ himself. If that dying one belongs to Christ, he or she is about to meet with joy the Savior who called himself "the light of the world" (John 8:12). I don't like driving through deep dark tunnels on mountain highways, but how amazing is that moment when we suddenly emerge into the almost blinding light of day.

In the suffering of death, it is true: the darkest part of the path meets the part most full of light. This was true on the cross as Jesus died for us, and because of his death for us, it is true as we die: as those in Christ are leaving this life, they are getting closer and closer to life and light that will never be taken away. We can take Paul at his word when he wrote that, even as his "outer self" was wasting away, his "inner self" was being renewed day by day (2 Cor. 4:16). Our renewal in Christ, as by his Spirit our old sinful selves are gradually and then finally transformed into his likeness, is a process that moves inexorably toward light and life.

When we die and go home to heaven the process will be complete: we will be finally and fully sanctified—holy and without sin—able to live in Christ's presence. What a hope! Add to that the glorious prospect of the final resurrection at Christ's second coming. "We shall be like him," writes the apostle John, "because we shall see him as he is" (1 John 3:2). No wonder Paul calls our earthly suffering a "light momentary affliction," in view of the hope that pulls us on toward "an eternal weight of glory beyond all comparison" (2 Cor. 4:17).

The glory of this heavenly hope shines brighter than anything in the world. It lights the way through death into eternity. We can hold out this hope for our aged and dying loved ones by reading and talking about God's Word, hearing and singing the hymns of the faith, listening to God's Word preached, sharing testimonies of faith . . . all the means we have so often mentioned in the course of this book. These means of hope are good to the end, to light up the way home. For loved ones who do not belong to Christ, or whose hearts we simply do not know, we can speak God's Word even in the final moments, calling them to faith—and we can and must trust the sovereign, merciful God who rules the universe. Our hope is in him alone.

This eternal hope is good not just for our aging and dying loved ones; it is good especially for us caregivers as well. We caregivers also need hope that lights up eternity. Death is a sudden departure; we on this side feel the absence of our loved ones the moment they have taken their last breath. We know they're gone, and we grieve. We grieve deeply.

How wonderful that the Bible takes time to comfort those who grieve the loss of loved ones in the Lord. That comfort grows from understanding and hoping in God's revelation of what is to come. As the apostle Paul encourages and instructs the Thessalonian believers in these matters, he explains that we who are still alive will see our believing loved ones again, for those who are "asleep" (i.e., those who have died) will take part in Jesus's return to earth; they will be resurrected first—and then we will join them. I will not dwell on all the details here, but we should read and store in our hearts the entire passage, overflowing with hope as it is:

> But we do not want you to be uninformed, brothers and sisters, about those who are asleep, that you may not grieve as others do who have no hope. For since we believe that Jesus died and rose again, even so, through Jesus, God will bring with him those who have fallen asleep. For this we declare to you by a word from the Lord, that we who are alive, who are left until the coming of the Lord, will not precede those who have fallen asleep. For the Lord himself will descend from heaven with a cry of command, with the voice of an archangel, and with the sound of the trumpet of God. And the dead in Christ will rise first. Then we who are alive, who are left, will be caught up together with them in the clouds to meet the Lord in the air, and so we will always be with the Lord. Therefore encourage one another with these words. (1 Thess. 4:13–18)

The Scriptures give hope that lights the way toward life after death, and they also give hope that allows those left behind to peer after their loved ones who have fallen asleep. That is how I felt when my father died: as if I were straining my eyes to see what he was seeing as he sat up and raised his arms. On this side of glory, we cannot see it—but we can be filled with the ultimate comfort of hope.

When Jesus saw that his disciples were sad to hear about his impending departure (his death, and then his ascension into heaven), he comforted them. "Let not your hearts be troubled," he said—and then he not only told them about his Father's house in heaven but also assured them that he was going to prepare a place for them there, and that he would come back and take them home to be with him (see John 14:1–3).

Peering after our dying loved ones often makes our eyesight better. We who are still alive cannot see those heavenly realities yet, but when we tread with an aging person close to the borders of heaven, close to the doorway, our spiritual eyes often grow sharper along with theirs.

One friend who, with her husband, cared for her mother until her death wrote this: "In the months preceding her death, the veil between here and eternity became thin; she saw things and spoke from that heavenly perspective—which was a huge blessing and encouragement to those who got to hear what she said. She was our amazing example of what communion, abiding, and oneness with Jesus looked like." In her dying, that elderly mother saw the light more clearly, and she helped the light shine more brightly for all who had the privilege of being with her.

Hope That Energizes

If we didn't know that we were preparing for realities that are absolutely amazing . . . that we have longed for . . . that we have been aiming for . . . we might be paralyzed by the approach of death. We caregivers in particular might not find the zeal to help our dying loved one on with songs and acts and words of hope. Many of us have entered the room of an elderly person where a caregiver is sitting and where the atmosphere feels lifeless and depressing.

Now, there will be many quiet moments of just sitting with elderly folks; it is good simply to be with them—not only when we're taking care of practical things but also when we are just letting them know that we care and that we are there. Children (or grandchildren) frequently want us adults to stay with them in their bedrooms as they go to sleep at night, for our very presence is comforting. It is often the same as aging folks approach death.

A caregiver has the opportunity, however, to bring the energy of hope into a room. Even in the quiet moments, it is possible to have a ready smile, or a song, or a good story, or a passage of Scripture—an acknowledgment that there is light just across the threshold of this room. Hope brings resources with it, because hope is focused on anticipating and preparing for what is ahead.

I've always loved the line in the Christmas lullaby "Away in a Manger" that asks God to "fit us for heaven, to live with thee there." Even a child can pray to get ready for heaven—how much more a person who knows he or she is close to the doorway. When we are preparing for a vacation to a beachfront resort, for example, our thoughts are occupied long beforehand with what clothes to pack, what activities to plan, and on and on. We imagine the sandy beach and that first dive into the ocean waves. We tell our travel companions about the region where we will be; we learn a bit about the language and the culture; we find the best restaurants. There is an energy to such planning. Hope gives this energy.

The energy of hope for life after death is the energy of preparing to meet the Lord Jesus. It is not physical but spiritual energy. It is actually less like the energy spent planning for a vacation and more like that spent planning for a trip to see a beloved spouse from whom we've been separated for far too long; those in the military, for example, might have a sense of it. Your thoughts and dreams are full of that one; you've read his or her letters over and over; you can't wait to see that dear face in the flesh. You make yourself as attractive and as ready as possible, to be pleasing to that loved one. You are energized by hope as you long for the day.

Examples help, but they pale in comparison to the eternal realities we are talking about. These realities should wake us up more and more, spiritually speaking, so that we do not give up aiming and hoping to the end—and so that we might help our loved ones to be renewed in their inner selves by real hope centered on Christ the risen Lord. My parents used to sing in a duet the hymn "Face to Face with Christ, My Savior":

Face to face with Christ, my Savior,
Face to face, what will it be
When with rapture I behold him,
Jesus Christ who died for me?[2]

J. I. Packer says it well in his little book *Finishing Our Course with Joy*, as he writes about what he himself truly lived out to the end. He warns against spiritual lethargy in the later years, when our bodies fail; he encourages zeal for the Lord, as much as is possible, even as bodies weaken physically. His final chapter acknowledges that what fuels this zeal is hope, unfailing hope in the Lord who created us to hope in him: "We humans are hopers by nature. Hope motivates, energizes, and drives us. It is natural to us to look ahead and long for any good things that we foresee. That is how God made us. It was always in his plan that we, his embodied rational creatures, should live our lives in this world looking forward to, and preparing for, something even better than we have known already."[3]

Sometimes an aging person helps us caregivers cultivate this hope in ourselves, as we watch and learn. Sometimes we must help an aging person cultivate hope, as we aim to turn their thoughts to the Lord and to the Bible's promises. Sometimes—often—we caregivers must ask others for help in encouraging an aging person to hope in the Lord.

It is crucial to keep remembering, as we have said many times in these chapters, that we cannot do this job alone. First, of course, we must pray and ask God's help, through his Spirit, who is ever at work though we cannot see him. But family and friends and pastors have their roles to play as well, and we should not fail to ask, and to embrace that help when it is there.

2. Carrie Ellis Breck, "Face to Face with Christ, My Savior," 1898.

3. J. I. Packer, *Finishing Our Course with Joy: Guidance from God for Engaging with Our Aging* (Wheaton, IL: Crossway, 2014), 79.

One of my friends exhibited amazing energy and planning alongside others in the months before her father's death. She is blessed with two siblings, and they all get along well—so they had a great head start in dealing with their dad's battle with the cancer that led to his death. (Their mother had already died.) In her notes from the last weeks of care, my friend wrote this counsel: "Talk about end of life; it is an open door to unspeakably great eternal things." They talked much with their father—about practical things and about the Lord and the hope of heaven.

But they didn't just talk: the three siblings organized a schedule that assigned each of them a week's care at a time, overlapping by one day of "precious" interaction and catching up. They researched various hospice care services and chose one—glad to find that hospice care would be covered by Medicare. One sibling worked on legal matters during his weeks there in their father's home, another on bills and upkeep, another on meal preparation; they all used their gifts.

Toward the end, the one with their dad sent updates each night to extended family (twenty of them), all of whom stayed up for that nightly email full of details, humor, sentiment, and encouragement in the Lord. Some of the grandchildren were able to pay last visits. Her father's life ended as my friend, her husband, and their two children were gathered close around him, thanking Grandpa for all he had done for them, praying and reading their favorite psalms out loud, and singing hymns (the final one was "He Leadeth Me"[4]). As their dad was slipping away, my friend

4. The final verse of this text written by J. H. Gilmore (1862) offers an amazing affirmation of hope:

> And when my task on earth is done,
> When, by thy grace, the victory's won,
> E'en death's cold wave I will not flee,
> Since God through Jordan leadeth me.

texted her siblings, "Closer to life," and then a few minutes later, "Home." One texted back, "Psalm 116:15—Precious in the sight of the Lord is the death of His saints."

This is a story full of hope at work: the family turned their heavenly hope into energetic earthly service as they worked together to usher their loved one into heaven.

Now, it's not always that well organized and harmonious. We don't all have the same resources and abilities. Each situation with a dying loved one is unique, and we give time and help as we are able. Sometimes we have no siblings to help; sometimes we have siblings who cannot or will not help. Extended family, fellow church members, friends, and neighbors are treasures in such times—and often they delight to help us. They can infuse hope into hard situations. Many of my mother's friends have done that for her and for me. During the hours with my mother in the hospital, it seemed that God kept bringing a pastor or a friend to visit just at the right time, with just the right psalm or prayer that we needed to hear.

Another dear friend wrote honestly about her ongoing struggles to let people help her care for her elderly mother: she wants her mother's care to be just right, to the very end. We all recognize that desire to control the process, that zeal to make it just what we believe it should be (as if we could). We think of ourselves as the hope our loved ones need (as if we were in the place of God). My friend acknowledged this "territorial" tendency in herself, recognizing that she may be preventing other people from having the opportunity to serve her mom; she may be stirring up resentment in others; she may not be allowing her mother to experience God's faithfulness as fully as she might, through many loving hands that bring help and hope.

Byron Peters calls elder care "a team sport, made up of family members, church friends, prayer partners, and financial and medical professionals who can work together for your loved one's physical and spiritual benefit (and your sanity!)."[5] And there is further benefit: every member of the "team" has the opportunity to witness God's faithfulness that sustains us in life and death.

It is good for us to learn that our hope in Christ turns us outward and ahead, with hearts stretched by the love of the Savior we're preparing to meet. Our hope grows as we humbly share it with those around us.

Hope That Grows

Hope grows as we share it—which means we focus on the substance of hope as presented in God's Word. We try to imagine the wonders of the promised new creation, with new bodies, a new heaven, and a new earth, all through the redeeming work of Christ. We can't wait to live without sin in us or around us. We read that God will wipe away every tear from our eyes "and death shall be no more, neither shall there be mourning, nor crying, nor pain anymore, for the former things have passed away" (Rev. 21:4). We ponder these glorious things to come, and our hope grows ever more large and clear.

But the source of our growing hope is ultimately the Lord God himself, the one seated on the throne in the midst of his new creation: God himself will dwell with us his people (see Rev. 21:3, 5). The Lord himself is the center of our hope; that is why our hope is sure. The triune God will reign over all, and we will be *with him*, in his glorious presence forever.

Because God's dwelling with his people is the climax of God's promises, we can experience this growing hope even now—for in Christ, God is with us. Jesus Christ is our Immanuel: literally, "God with us" (Matt. 1:23). Jesus Christ the Word "became flesh

5. Byron Peters, *Caring for an Aging Parent: Honoring as You Serve* (Greensboro, NC: New Growth Press, 2020), 11.

and dwelt among us" (John 1:14). Jesus died for us, rose from the dead, ascended to heaven, and then sent his very Spirit to abide with us and to guide us into all truth, until Jesus comes again (see John 16:7–15). We believers know Christ's presence even now through his Spirit, and we know Christ's presence more and more as the Spirit helps the Word of God grow in us richly. One day, we will be with him fully—but, until then, we live in his presence with ever-growing faith and hope.

As we share true biblical hope with the aging ones for whom we care, then, we are sharing not simply the reality of a promise for the future but the reality of God himself, the God who came to us in Christ his Son. What that Son did to save us is our only lasting hope, the hope we will be wondering over and singing about forever in heaven—even as we begin to sing about it now. We will never get to the end of it. Worthy is the Lamb who was slain for the salvation of God's people from every tribe and nation . . . that is the song of heaven (see Rev. 5:9–10). Psalm 71 explains why our hope keeps growing and growing:

> I will hope continually
>   and will praise you yet more and more.
> My mouth will tell of your righteous acts,
>   of your deeds of salvation all the day,
>   for their number is past my knowledge. (vv. 14–15)

God's "deeds of salvation," accomplished finally in Christ, are so great that we will never comprehend such greatness. We will continue to learn more and more of him, and so we will "hope continually," praising him "yet more and more."

At the end of this book on caring for our aging loved ones, we should return to the rooms in which they wait. When I began writing this book, my mother was ninety-six; as I finish, she is ninety-seven. She hopes and longs for heaven. And yet she is waiting with faith, aiming to encourage and pray faithfully for friends and loved ones near and far. I continue to make that regular trip to be with her, pulling up in front of the assisted-living facility in Lancaster County, Pennsylvania, across from the farms and cornfields that keep changing with the seasons, from green and full to brown and stubbly and back again.

As I turn my rental car into my favorite parking space (the only place where I allow myself to use her handicapped parking permit!), I stop again. My mind is full of the heavenly realities about which I have been writing, and I think with wonder that the little full-of-stuff apartment I'm about to enter is right next door to heaven. The frail white-haired mom I'm about to spend time with is an eternal soul, dearly loved by the God of the universe, who has written her days in his book—and who has given her to me to honor as my mother, all her days.

I have arrived to help her in her time of need, and yet I'm more aware than ever that God is her true help; he sees her suffering better than I can, and he has promised to be her help and my help to the end. He has promised much more: the glories of heaven, face-to-face with Jesus, alongside loved ones sorely missed. This retirement community is a home, if we could see it, where huge, earth-shattering things are happening all the time, as eternal souls are getting ready and then stepping through the doorway into brilliant glory. Let me not be oblivious. May I have faith to see.

It is good to end with hope, true hope, grounded in God and in his Word. We need this hope, for some of these rooms are dark. God sent his Son to show us this hope, and we see it most clearly as we look to the cross and then to the empty tomb. Through the Scriptures, we see the Savior who suffered and died, taking on all our sin in our place. Through the Scriptures, we see the Savior who rose from the dead, conquering sin and death for us and opening the way for us to follow him into resurrection life. His path through death into life shows us the way of faith, trusting in his death on our behalf and hoping with certainty to live with him forever.

We're walking toward the light as we follow Jesus through that doorway. At the end of the day, here is what we need to know—or, better yet, *whom* we need to know—in order to care well for our aging and dying loved ones: Jesus, the way, the truth, and the life.

Let's go in. Let's go in to these rooms with eyes and hearts open. Let's be those who "make some return to their parents, for this is pleasing in the sight of God" (1 Tim. 5:4). Let's make good return. Let's bring light. Let's fit ourselves for heaven in the process, aiming above all to please our heavenly Father, whom we also will meet before too long. In a breath's time, we caregivers will be the aging, dying ones, if Christ does not return first. Fit us for heaven, Lord. Fit all of us for heaven, to live with Thee there.

Bibliography

Betters, Sharon W., and Susan Hunt. *Aging with Grace: Flourishing in an Anti-Aging Culture*. Wheaton, IL: Crossway, 2021.

Bunyan, John. *The Pilgrim's Progress from This World to That Which Is to Come*. Philadelphia: Porter & Coates, 1893.

Carmichael, Amy. *Mountain Breezes: The Collected Poems of Amy Carmichael*. Fort Washington, PA: Christian Literature Crusade, 1999.

Carson, D. A., *Memoirs of an Ordinary Pastor: The Life and Reflections of Tom Carson*. Wheaton, IL: Crossway, 2008.

Davis, Bill. *Departing in Peace: Biblical Decision-Making at the End of Life*. Phillipsburg, NJ: P&R Publishing, 2017.

Elliot, Elisabeth. *A Chance to Die: The Life and Legacy of Amy Carmichael*. Old Tappan, NJ: Fleming H. Revell, 1987.

Gawande, Atul. *Being Mortal: Medicine and What Matters in the End*. New York: Picador, 2017.

Oliphint, K. Scott, and Sinclair B. Ferguson. *If I Should Die before I Wake: Help for Those Who Hope for Heaven*. Grand Rapids: Baker Books, 1995.

Packer, J. I. *Finishing Our Course with Joy: Guidance from God for Engaging with Our Aging*. Wheaton, IL: Crossway, 2014.

Peters, Byron. *Caring for an Aging Parent: Honoring as You Serve*. Greensboro, NC: New Growth Press, 2020.

Prime, Derek. *A Good Old Age: An A to Z of Loving and Following the Lord Jesus in Later Years*. Leyland, UK: 10Publishing, 2017.

Ryken, Leland. *40 Favorite Hymns on the Christian Life: A Closer Look at Their Spiritual and Poetic Meaning*. Phillipsburg, NJ: P&R Publishing, 2019.

Tolstoy, Leo. *The Death of Iván Ilých*. In *Eleven Modern Short Novels*, edited by Leo Hamalian and Edmond L. Volpe. 2nd ed. New York: Putnam, 1970, 3–61.

Kathleen B. Nielson (PhD, Vanderbilt University) is an author and speaker who loves working with women in studying the Scriptures. She has taught literature, directed women's Bible studies in local churches, and served as director of The Gospel Coalition's Women's Initiatives from 2010 to 2017. She and her husband, Niel, make their home partly in Wheaton, Illinois, and partly in Jakarta, Indonesia, where Niel helps to lead a network of Christian schools and universities. They have three sons, three daughters-in-law, and a growing number of grandchildren.

Also by Kathleen Nielson

Poetic prayers by Kathleen Nielson bring praises and petitions to the Lord who knows and loves our children perfectly. Covering their spiritual well-being, physical needs, and character growth, the prayers are accompanied by brief reflections from Kathleen as well as Scripture passages for meditation.

"I know of no other guide to parental prayer like Nielson's tender, insightful, gospel-rich, and loving little book. Read it and you will find yourself praying for new things for your children in new ways."
—**Paul David Tripp**, Author, *New Morning Mercies* and *Parenting*

"It can be tough to pause and intentionally pray for our children prayers that align with the concerns of God laid out in his Word. This is where Kathleen's prayers come alongside us in our weariness, anxiety, and ambitions. These prayers are worth sitting with, chewing on, and praying. I will be using and sharing this resource for many years to come."
—**Quina Aragon**, Author, *Love Made* and *Love Gave*

Did you find this book helpful?
Consider writing a review online.
We appreciate your feedback!

Or write to P&R at editorial@prpbooks.com
with your comments. We'd love to hear from you.